GROSS
GUIDES
TO PSYCHOLOGY
OCR A2

SANDRA HARDERN
SARAH MIDDLETON
RICHARD GROSS

HODDER
EDUCATION
AN HACHETTE UK COMPANY

Photo credits and permissions

The authors and publishers would like to thank the following for the use of photography in this volume:

Figure 1.1 © Gina Sanders – Fotolia; Figure 4.1 © windzepher – Fotolia; Figure 4.2 © Sven Bähren – Fotolia; Figure 5.2 © Kati Molin – Fotolia; Figure 5.3 © Zsolt Bota Finna – Fotolia; Figure 5.4 Funhaler is a Avita Medical product (www.avitamedical.com); Figure 6.1 © Grecaud Paul – Fotolia; Figure 6.2 © Moritz Wussow – Fotolia; Figure 6.3 © WILL & DENI MCINTYRE/SCIENCE PHOTO LIBRARY; Figure 6.4 © alessandrozocc – Fotolia; Figure 8.2 © Nikolai Sorokin – Fotolia; Figure 8.4 © Monkey Business – Fotolia; Figure 8.5 © ermess – Fotolia; Figure 8.9 ©WELLCOME DEPT. OF COGNITIVE NEUROLOGY/SCIENCE PHOTO LIBRARY; Figure 9.1 © karaboux – Fotolia; Figure 10.1 © Neil Tingle/actionplus sports images; Figure 13.3 © Dmitry Nikolaev – Fotolia; Figure 13.7 © Maxim_Kazmin – Fotolia; Figure 13.8 © smart.art – Fotolia; Figure 13.9 © Vivid Pixels – Fotolia.

We would also like to thank the following:

Table 2.2 is adapted from Canter, D., Alison, L.J., Alison, E. and Wentink, N. (2004) 'The organised/disorganised typology of serial murder: myth or model?' *Psychology, Public Policy and the Law*, 10 (3), 293–320. Published by the American Psychological Association and adapted with permission.

Table 4.1 is adapted from Dooley, E. (1990) 'Prison suicide in England and Wales, 1972-87'. *The British Journal of Psychiatry*, 156: 40-45 and is used with permission.

Figure 8.7 is taken from Freeman, D., Garety, P.A. Kuipers, E., Fowler, D. and Bebbington P.E. (2002) 'A cognitive model of persecutory delusions'. *British Journal of Clinical Psychology*, 41, 331–47 © 2002 The British Psychological Society and published by Wiley. Reproduced with permission.

Table 11.4 is adapted from Zajonc, R.B., Heingartner, A. and Herman, E.M. (1969) 'Social enhancement and impairment of performance in the cockroach.' *Journal of Personality and Social Psychology*, 13 (2), 83–92. Published by the American Psychological Association and adapted with permission.

Every effort has been made to obtain necessary permission with reference to copyright material. The publishers apologise if inadvertently any sources remain unacknowledged and will be glad to make the necessary arrangements at the earliest opportunity.

Acknowledgements

The publishers would like to thank the authors of the book; Sandra Hardern (Forensic, and Sport and Exercise Psychology), Sarah Middleton (Health and Clinical Psychology) and Richard Gross. We would also like to thank Moira Donald and Louise Ellerby-Jones whose material formed the Research Methods section.

Orders: please contact Bookpoint Ltd, 130 Milton Park, Abingdon, Oxon OX14 4SB. Telephone: (44) 01235 827720. Fax: (44) 01235 400454. Lines are open from 9.00 - 5.00, Monday to Saturday, with a 24 hour message answering service. You can also order through our website www.hoddereducation.co.uk

If you have any comments to make about this, or any of our other titles, please send them to educationenquiries@hodder.co.uk

British Library Cataloguing in Publication Data
A catalogue record for this title is available from the British Library

ISBN: 9781444168143

Published 2012
Impression number   10 9 8 7 6 5 4 3 2
Year   2016, 2015, 2014, 2013, 2012

Hachette UK's policy is to use papers that are natural, renewable and recyclable products and made from wood grown in sustainable forests. The logging and manufacturing processes are expected to conform to the environmental regulations of the country of origin.

Illustrations by Barking Dog Art and DC Graphic Design Limited, Swanley Village, Kent
Typeset by DC Graphic Design Limited, Swanley Village, Kent.

Printed in Dubai for Hodder Education, An Hachette UK Company, 338 Euston Road, London NW1 3BH by Oriental Press

Contents

CHAPTER 8: DISORDERS

SPORT AND EXERCISE PSYCHOLOGY   62

CHAPTER 9: SPORT AND THE INDIVIDUAL

CHAPTER 10: SPORT PERFORMANCE

CHAPTER 11: SOCIAL PSYCHOLOGY OF SPORT

CHAPTER 12: EXERCISE PSYCHOLOGY

CHAPTER 13: RESEARCH METHODS

How to use this book

This book will help you revise for your OCR A2 Psychology exams. It is designed so that you can use it alongside any appropriate textbook, including Richard Gross's *Psychology: The Science of Mind and Behaviour*.

Each of the Key Studies are covered in the following way:

Results of the study are shown clearly alongside.

The outline of the study giving details about the background, aims, sample, method and procedure.

Cowpe, C. (1989) Chip pan fire prevention 1976–1988

Aim: To demonstrate that advertising can make a valuable contribution to reducing the number of chip pan fire accidents.

Background: In the 1970s and early 1980s people commonly cooked chips at home in an open pan. These pans frequently caught fire.

Sample/participants: TV viewers living in the Yorkshire Granada, Central, Tyne Tees and London regions where the adverts were shown were contacted.

Method: Field experiment.

Procedure: A TV campaign was produced with two 60-second commercials entitled 'Unattendance' and 'Overfilling'. Both showed the initial cause of the fire and then the actions needed to put it out: 1) Turn off the heat; 2) Cover with a damp cloth; 3) Leave the pan to cool down.

Results: The overall results showed a net decline in fires of between 7% and 25% in twelve months with the greatest effect immediately after the campaign. Advertising awareness and recall also improved across the areas studied, suggesting that fires were being prevented by greater awareness of the risk and where a fire did occur it was contained and did not require the attendance of the fire brigade.

Evaluation: This field experiment is high in ecological validity. People were at home so there were no demand characteristics. However, we do not know if the message was spread by the advertisements in every case because there is no control over who watched them.

Debates: This could be considered as a situational explanation rather than a dispositional one. Once people knew what to do, they could act accordingly. Usefulness – the findings are useful because they show that if you want to change an unhealthy behaviour it is important to explain what to do rather than just what to avoid..

Accompanying material will help you evaluate the study and highlight any relevant debates associated with that study, to help you get those top marks!

The research methods are also covered in a colourful and exciting way, to help you retain and recall the information.

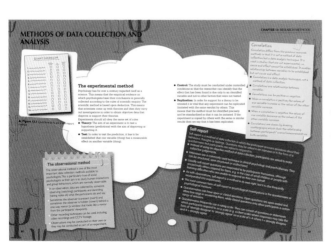

FORENSIC PSYCHOLOGY

1. Turning to crime (see pp. 4–9)

Why do some people commit crime, while others do not? What is the possible impact of upbringing, cognitions and biological influences on criminal activity?

1. **Upbringing:** presents research (and a theory) which are essentially interested in social context and trying to identify factors which are linked with offending behaviour, particularly risk and protective factors associated with upbringing (e.g. having convicted parents). The importance of learning from others is put forward and the effects of poverty, disadvantage, lifestyles, family/school bonds and parental monitoring are also considered.

2. **Cognition:** our thoughts are generally acknowledged to determine our actions. A critical research question is, 'Do offenders think differently to non-offenders?' Offending might be considered one outcome of 'faulty thinking' and/or a lack of moral development. This sub-topic also considers how offenders attribute blame for certain types of crime (violent, sexual and property).

3. **Biology:** those implicated in criminal behaviour are considered here, such as brain dysfunction, genes, gender and evolutionary explanations. The developing brain is not fully formed in adolescence (when criminal activity often peaks) and other biological factors (e.g. a low resting heart rate) are identified and discussed as influential factors, as is the evolutionary basis for risk-taking in males.

2. Making a case (see pp. 10–15)

How reliable is eye-witness testimony? Do interrogation techniques affect the likelihood of confession and securing convictions? Can profiling help apprehend offenders?

1. **Interviewing witnesses:** covers research investigating which facial features eyewitnesses attend to (with implications for computer-aided 'photofit' procedures for suspect identification); how weapons involved in the commission of a crime affect memory of the event and an interviewing technique (the cognitive interview) and its positive affect on information retrieval.

2. **Interviewing suspects:** covers research into police officers' ability to detect lies; a confrontational interview technique (Reid's 'Nine-steps') used to obtain confessions (which assumes suspects' guilt) and different types of false confession (voluntary, coerced-compliant, coerced internalised).

3. **Offender profiling:** considers the reliability of typologies of organised and disorganised offenders (do offenders fit neatly into one or other category?); developments in profiling (e.g. small-space analysis and geographic profiling) and the case of John Duffy (a serial offender convicted for the rape and murder of women).

3. Reaching a verdict (see pp. 16–21)

What factors impact on a juror's decision making and to what extent does the group affect this process and ultimately the verdict?

1. **Persuading a jury:** considers the effect the order the evidence is presented to the jury has on guilty verdicts; the effect of expert witness testimony on jurors' verdicts and confidence in their decisions and whether evidence ruled inadmissible by a judge can, in fact, be disregarded by jurors.

2. **Witness appeal:** the attractiveness of the defendant and the victim is considered in terms of the impact on jurors' guilty verdicts; the effect of witness confidence on jurors' guilty verdicts and whether courtroom practices (e.g. the use of shields or video links with child witnesses) has a positive or negative impact on jurors' verdicts.

3. **Reaching a verdict:** jurors are part of a social group and jury discussion/decision making is theorised to go through the same or similar processes identified in general social psychological research. Conformity, majority influence and minority influence from experimental research are established as impacting on an individual's decision making in group situations.

4. After a guilty verdict (see pp. 22-27)

Do employment programmes prior to release from prison have an effect on an offender's likelihood of re-offending? What is the impact of alternatives to imprisonment? How useful/effective are treatment programmes used with convicted offenders in the prison system?

1. **Imprisonment:** research considers the effect of planning for release (e.g. via employment programmes) on reducing re-offending. Depression and the risk of suicide in prison are also investigated and a review of the past 25 years of the USA prison system and future policy suggestions are presented.

2. **Alternatives to imprisonment:** research considers offenders' experiences of probation and investigates its usefulness; restorative justice is considered in the light of its effectiveness on recidivism or re-offending; investigating possible racial prejudice in sentencing considers whether offenders with more stereotypically black features are more likely to receive the death penalty than offenders with less stereotypically black features.

3. **Treatment programmes:** cognitive skills, anger management and ear acupuncture (used on offenders in the prison system) are evaluated in terms of their effectiveness/usefulness, especially in the light of possibly reducing re-offending/recidivism.

UPBRINGING

Farrington, D.P. *et al.* (2006) The Cambridge Study in Delinquent Development

Aim: This research seeks to document the start, duration and end of offending (and anti-social) behaviour; to identify risk and protective factors and the influence of family background on offending, and to advance knowledge about conviction careers up to age 50.

Sample/participants: 411 boys, aged 8–9 (born 1953–54), from six East London state schools; 87% white, mainly working class and of British origin (and boys' parents and teachers).

Method/procedure: A longitudinal survey (started 1961) with data gathered from interviews and criminal records data. Interviews conducted: i) at school at age 8, 10 and 14; ii) in research office at age 16, 18 and 21; iii) in homes at *c.* 25, 32 and *c.* 48 years. At the age of 48, 394 males were still alive and 365 (93 %) were interviewed. Parental interviews conducted when boys aged 8–14/15 (in the home). Teachers completed questionnaires when boys were aged 8, 10, 12 and 14.

Conclusion: As most prolific offenders start early, suggests ten-year-olds should be targeted.

Evaluation: Large sample, some subject attrition, but can still be considered reliable. Self-reports from interview are liable to socially desirable responses/lying (affecting validity). More objective data from official records.

Issues: Longitudinal study allows for development of behaviour over time to be identified/more reliable than a snapshot.

Debates: Main risk factors can illustrate understanding of the nurture debate. Very useful to target resources (e.g. education programmes, parenting classes). Social determinism (e.g. convicted family).

Perspectives: Psychodynamic – early experiences (e.g. convicted parent) may affect later life. Behaviourist – observation may result in imitation (link: AS Bandura study).

Results:

1. 41% were convicted for standard offences (e.g. theft, burglary, vandalism, drug abuse) between 10 and 50 years old, with the average conviction career lasting from age 19 to 28 years (average of five convictions).
2. Offences peak at age 17.
3. Most important childhood (age 8–10) risk factors for later offending were measures of: family criminality, daring/risk-taking, poor school attainment, poverty, poor parenting. Early onset, 10–13 year-olds, commit more crimes on average (9 compared to 6 in 14–16-year-olds).
4. Chronic offenders (7% of sample) commit over 50% of officially recorded offences and share commonalities (more likely to have convicted parent, high daring, delinquent sibling, young mother, low popularity, disrupted family and from large family); average conviction career from age 14 to 35.
5. Nearly half of all self-reported offences were committed by unconvicted men; for convicted men, for every conviction there was an average of 22 self-reported offences.
6. Desisters no different in 'life success' measures (e.g. satisfactory mental health and employment history, no self-report of crime/no convictions in last five years) from unconvicted.

(NB. 1993 findings: 40% of males convicted up to age 40 and 28% of fathers, 13% of mothers, 43% of brothers, 12% of sisters, 9% of wives.)

Sutherland, E.H. (1947): Theory of Differential Association

This theory, summarised in a book, comprises nine principles, including:

1. The more an individual associates with criminals, compared to time associating with non-criminals, the more likely it is that an individual will offend – this is differential association.

Some other principles:

2. Criminal behaviour is learned (i.e. not inherited or resulting from some biological condition).

3. It is learned in interaction with others (i.e. social learning*).

4. The largest influence on criminal behaviour is intimate personal groups (these are most likely to be family, friends/peers) – Sutherland considered the influence of (impersonal) media unimportant.

5. Learning includes techniques involved in commission of crime as well as attitudes/beliefs.

Results:

1. c. 45% of males and c. 31% of females have committed at least one of studied crimes (violence, vandalism, shoplifting, burglary and theft).

2. c. 10% of males and c. 4% of females have committed serious crime (robbery, theft, burglary).

3. High-frequency offenders commit a wide range of crimes and the most serious crimes.

4. Offenders more often drunk/use drugs than non-offenders.

Risk factors, which strongly affected involvement in crime are: a) individual characteristics/dispositions (poor self-control, antisocial values, low levels of shame) categorised as 'propensity-induced' offenders and b) lifestyles (high risk spend a lot of time with peers in public settings, using drugs/alcohol and truanting from school), categorised as 'lifestyle dependent'.

Protective factors include strong family and school bonds (including good attendance), with good parental monitoring.

Wikstrom, P-O. and Tajfel, H. (2003): The Peterborough Youth Study

Background/aim: This is one of a series of longitudinal studies of Social Contexts of Pathways into Crime (SCoPiC) and it set out to test a range of factors (poverty, disadvantage, substance abuse, etc.) and to identify which were the most significant predictors of criminal behaviour (and to investigate the interaction between individual life-style risk and its influence on offending).

Sample/participants: 1957, 14–15-year-olds from 13 state schools in the Peterborough area.

Method/procedure: Cross-sectional, snapshot study. The questionnaire study (conducted 2000–01), response rate c. 92%, followed up by a random sample of 339 (20%) who were interviewed about a week's activities which they had logged, response rate c. 83%. Data on neighbourhood disadvantage obtained from the 1991 Census.

Evaluation: Large, reliable sample, although age and geographically specific; however, targeting this age group is appropriate given early onset of offending. Self-reports liable to socially desirable responses/lying (question validity).

Debates: As the study investigates a wide range of factors it is less reductionist; however, as it does not investigate (for example) biological factors it is still somewhat reductionist. Very useful for identifying predictive factors for offendin behaviour, although this risks 'labelling' (link: AS Rosenhan study) and the dangers of self-fulfilling prophecy. Nurture/social determinism influences on criminal activity.

Extend

Research PADS (Peterborough Adolescent Development Study).

Evaluation: Theory needs rigorous testing in order to establish its credibility/usefulness – difficult to test. Sutherland's discounting the influence of media indicates this aspect of theory is out of date.

Perspectives: Behaviourist – can be illustrated/evidenced by Sutherland's assertion that criminal behaviour is learned, and learned in interaction with others in intimate personal groups. From this we can infer imitation (*Link: AS study, Bandura; Bandura's SLT).

Debates: Nurture (see above). Reductionist does not take into account influences of media and technology ('loners' can access and learn information via computers). Intimate personal groups could be considered as social determinants of offending; however, individuals have free will.

Exam tip

Individual characteristics that may predispose someone to criminal activity, like lack of self-control, allows you to speculate about biological factors (e.g. ADHD).

COGNITION

Yochelson, S. and Samenow, S. (1976) A study of thinking patterns in criminals

Background/aim: To investigate whether criminals think differently to non-criminals.

Sample/participants: Began with 255 criminals (*c.* half had pleaded not guilty by reason of insanity and institutionalised, *c.* half convicted criminals, not in mental hospital, referred to authors by outside agencies, e.g. courts; only 30 completed all planned interviews).

Method/procedure: Longitudinal study over 14 years, conducted by two doctors working in a mental hospital, using interviews based on Freudian therapy attempting to find root cause of offending in early life; focus of therapy changed over time to investigate thinking processes/cognitions. No control group.

Results:
52 (or 40 in 1984 study) thinking errors were reported as being identified in the criminal personality, which fall into three main categories:
1. Crime-related thinking errors, e.g. 'optimistic fantasising' (where an offender tends to focus on the likely rewards with no regard for possible deterrents) and lying;
2. Automatic thinking errors, e.g. lack of empathy and trust and failure to accept personal obligations/ think of themselves as a victim;
3. Criminal thinking patterns, which typically exhibit the offenders' need for power and control, combined with fear.
Authors conclude criminals are essentially in control of their lives and that offending is a result of choices made. They tend to have distorted self-image and typically deny responsibility.

Evaluation: The lack of a **control** group allows no confirmation that these thinking patterns exist **only** in offenders; however, this did not start out as a research project. Validity problems (i.e. socially desirable responses led to the change in focus) and subject attrition means very small sample (that completed interviews/therapy) is unreliable. Clinical (semi-structured) interviews and longitudinal nature of study means cannot be replicated to check for reliability and data is liable to interpretation bias.

Perspectives: The research started out looking for root causes of criminal behaviour in early life (psychodynamic).

Debates: Criminal thinking could be considered to be socially determined by learning from others (upbringing, peers, etc.); however, could argue offenders make a choice (free-will).

Usefulness: Subject attrition, validity issues and a lack of a control group means this cannot be considered very useful; however, cognitive skills programmes could be used to challenge irrational thinking (e.g. optimistic fantasising).

▲ **Figure 1.1** Yochelson and Samenow looked at whether criminals think differently to non-criminals

Extend

Cornish and Clarke's (2006) application of Rational Choice Theory argues that criminal behaviour arises out of a choice made after weighing 'pros' and 'cons', i.e., it is purposive with the intention to derive some benefit (money, reward, status, power, fun, excitement, physiological release, sexual gratification, etc.). Used to evidence understanding of free-will debate.

Kohlberg, L. (1963) Moral development in children

Background/aim: Heavily influenced by Piaget's stages of development, Kohlberg aimed to find evidence to support his theory that moral development progresses through stages.

Sample/participants: 72 boys from Chicago, aged 10, 13 and 16 (half in each group upper-middle class, half lower to lower-middle class), comparable in

Gudjohnnson, G.H. and Bownes, I. (2002) Attribution of blame and crime type

Background/aim: To investigate the possible relationship between type of offence and offenders' attributions about their criminal behaviour and to make comparisons with previous research on an English sample of convicted offenders.

Sample/participants: 80 convicted offenders serving sentences in Northern Ireland. 20 violent offenders (e.g. homicide and GBH), mean age of 29. 40 sex offenders (rapists, paedophiles and other sexual assault), paedophiles mean age 41, others mean age 28. 20 property offenders (e.g. theft, burglary), mean age 29.

Method/procedure: Questionnaire (Gudjohnnson-Bownes Attribution Inventory, GBAI) with 42 items (identifying i) offence; ii) attribution of blame – internal/external, iii) mental element and iv) guilt). Internal attributions (attribute cause of behaviour to themselves) and external (attribute cause to a range of social factors/pressures within environment). An example of a 'mental-element' would be 'I was depressed', while 'guilt' considers whether remorse is expressed or not.

Results: 'Sex offenders' expressed the most remorse, followed by 'violent' offenders. There was little difference across offence types regarding 'mental element' and highest scores on external attributions were from violent offenders and lowest for sex offenders. Results are consistent with English findings.

Evaluation: A serious limitation of self-report measures from offenders concerns validity as socially desirable responses/lying can be used to manipulate improved conditions, access to resources, etc.
(NB. In fact, prison psychologists working with sex offender programmes have previously reported a lack of internal attributions and offenders blaming the victim.)
Usefulness: Identifying attributions can allow specific targeting of resources, e.g. offenders making internal attributions might be more open to rehabilitation/treatment programmes (e.g. cognitive behavioural therapy). However, question usefulness given validity problems.
Link: Attribution theory and Locus of Control (Rotter, 1966).

Results: Kohlberg's theory outlined three levels of morality: Pre-morality, Conventional morality and Post-conventional morality, each with two stages. Results confirmed that younger boys were operating at the earlier stages of morality (Stage 1 out of fear of punishment; Stage 2 for personal gain). Older boys typically operated at later stages (Stage 3 doing right to be 'good'; Stage 4 obeying laws out of duty). Findings provide support for a stage theory of moral development.

Additional: Later research by Kohlberg conducted in different countries/cultures (UK, USA, Mexico, Taiwan, Turkey, Yucatan) confirmed stage theory across cultures.

IQ (and 24 16-year-old delinquents; 24 6-year-olds and 50 boys and girls aged 13 from near Boston).

Method/procedure: Interviews, tape-recorded (two hours' long, with 10 hypothetical moral dilemmas to solve, e.g. the most famous is the Heinz dilemma). Longitudinal aspect as some boys were followed up in later work at three-yearly intervals (up to age 30–36).

Evaluation: There are many limitations: 1. gender biased sample; 2. the fact that it is essentially a theory of **moral thinking**; 3. validity must be questioned given the use of self-reports, where socially desirable responses are likely to operate and also given both the length of interviews and the difficult nature of the dilemmas, particularly with the younger participants (and therefore also question its usefulness – debates).
Debates: Stage theories can be considered as having some physiological maturational basis (link: Piaget's developmental stage theory), nature debate, although could argue that we learn morals from our main caregivers' learning – nurture.

BIOLOGY

Raine, A. *et al.* (2002) The development of anti-social and aggressive behaviour in children

Background/aim: Raine, well known for his murderers' brains study (1997) has conducted an extensive review of research to identify (see title above).

Sample/participants: Varied (small and large), not geographically specific (although mainly from western, industrialised societies), wide variety of age ranges.

Method/procedure: Review of research articles on biological bases of anti-social and aggressive behaviour in children. Cross-sectional and longitudinal studies, many ruling out a wide range of potentially confounding variables (e.g. low IQ, poor academic ability, etc.) Selective focus on low autonomic functioning, prefrontal deficits and early health factors.

Evaluation: Can infer a respectable researcher would identify an appropriate range of published research articles which have scientific standing (therefore fairly reliable); however, cannot eliminate the possibility of researcher bias in the review process. Variation in sample sizes means reliability could be questioned, but many studies replicated and 'elimination' of confounding variables results in greater reliability.

Debates: There is a danger of offering only biological deterministic and reductionist explanations of offending behaviour.

Usefulness: Research suggests that early health intervention (e.g. regarding smoking, eating well during pregnancy) can potentially reduce later problems. Predictors which allow early identification must be useful; however, the danger is labelling someone as violent/aggressive (link with AS Rosenhan study), leading to 'self-fulfilling prophecy'.

Results:
1. A low resting heart rate is identified as a predictor of someone who is fearless/seeks stimulation and excitement (this is the best-replicated biological correlate of anti-social and aggressive behaviour; six different countries, e.g. England, New Zealand, Germany).
2. Structural and functional deficits found in pre-frontal lobe (brain), e.g. reduced blood flow and reduced glucose, are related to anti-social and aggressive behaviour often characterised by a lack of inhibitory control (from neuropsychological, neurological and brain-imaging studies).
3. Birth complications (e.g. lack of oxygen, forceps delivery and pre-eclampsia) are selectively associated with later violent behaviour (interaction with maternal rejection).
4. Significant link between smoking during pregnancy and later conduct disorder/violent offending.
5. Deficiencies in nutrition (findings somewhat controversial) but aggression and anti-social behaviour have been associated with food additives and deficiencies in iron, vitamins and protein.

Extend

Rowe states categorically 'there is no gene for crime'; however, you can argue that some genetic variation (e.g. high levels of testosterone) may be implicated with aggressive behaviour/ violent crime (but not for other crime types like fraud). Biological factors not covered e.g. brain abnormality (Charles Whitman's tumour pressing on the amygdala, responsible for controlling aggressive urges) and brain damage (Phineas Gage's accident where a bolt was blown through his jaw and into the pre-frontal lobe of his brain) are worth outlining as additional (possible) contributing factors to offending.

Results: Tests revealed a point mutation in the X chromosome of the gene responsible for production of monoamine oxidase A (MAOA – involved in serotonin metabolism). Males showed disturbed aggression regulation. Aggressive behaviour usually triggered by anger (usually out of proportion to provocation). Other abnormal behaviour documented: rape/attempted rape, stabbing, arson, exhibitionism and voyeurism.

Brunner, H.G. *et al.* (1993) Genetic abnormality and violent behaviour

Background: An early study (Price *et al.*, 1966) seemed to offer that genetic abnormality was strongly implicated in violent crime (the XYY syndrome); however, Witkin's later Danish study (1976) discounted this explanation and drew attention to lower intelligence as a more important factor (infer link to low school attainment).

Aim: to investigate genetic abnormality and violent behaviour.

Wilson, M. and Daly, M. (1997) Homicide rates and life expectancy

Background: Evolutionary explanations of criminal behaviour argue that 'more risky' and/or aggressive behaviour in males can be understood in terms of competition for mates, food and ultimately survival. Impulsiveness and risk-taking have been identified in research already and this study investigates the relationship between life expectancy and homicide rates. 'Risk-taking' is seen as a characteristic of male behaviour and is most likely to occur in a social context of peers (Wilson & Daly, 1985).

Aim: See method/procedure below.

Sample/participants: From 77 relatively stable community areas, Chicago (infer a large sample).

Method/procedure: A correlation study investigating the relationships between a) life expectancy and homicide rates and b) life expectancy and income inequality using demographic data from Illinois Department of Public Health (1988–93), police records and population census data 1990.

Results: strong negative correlations (p < 0.0001) a) −0.88 and b) −0.75. Homicide rates per 100,000 (across 77 areas in Chicago) ranged from 1.3 to 156 and life expectancy ranged from c. 54–77 years old.

Discussion of results:
a) Authors question whether young men expecting to live shorter lives (high homicide rate neighbourhoods) engaged in more risky behaviour to gain (short-term) rewards;
b) Poverty can be understood as a motivating factor in offending.

Evaluation: Correlations do not allow the establishment of cause and effect. The (inferred) large sample is reliable and the variety of data from census, police and school records is not liable to subjective interpretation and therefore valid and also reliable.
Debates: (biological) determinism and nature. Both the research and the explanations offered are reductionist, as a range of social or cognitive factors likely to be involved in offending are not considered. Nurture: young men seeing relatives/friends die young.
Links: Freud and Ethological theory consider aggression as innate (nature debate).

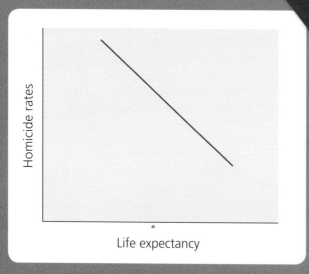

▲ **Figure 1.2** The relationship between homicide rates and life expectancy (negative correlation)

Sample/participants: 5 males from a Netherlands family (with syndrome of X-linked borderline mental retardation and abnormal violent behaviour); only one completed regular primary education (+ detailed case histories of three more affected males).

Method/procedure: Blood samples (to isolate DNA) and analysis of urine samples over 24 hours (and some 'clinical' case study behavioural material reported by family).

Evaluation/usefulness: The very small sample is unreliable and as not all males in this family were affected by associated violent behaviour the findings cannot be generalised, nor can they be considered very useful.
Debates: This research can be used to illustrate the weaknesses of using biologically deterministic and reductionist explanations of criminal behaviour.

Bruce, V. (Frowd) *et al.* (2007) Internal and external features in facial recognition

Background: Familiar faces are more reliably recognised than unfamiliar, regardless of identification conditions (e.g. lighting).

Experiment 1:

Aim: To investigate the relative recognisability of internal (eyes, nose, mouth, brows) and external (head shape, hair, ears) features.

Sample/participants: 30 staff and students; Stirling university, paid £2 to sort composites, gender balanced, aged 18–60 (mean age 29).

Method/procedure: Laboratory experiment (independent measures design). Set of ten composite/target celebrity colour photos (e.g. Ben Affleck); participants tested individually; randomly assigned to one of three composites (whole (face/head), internal or external features). Task: to view composites produced using different UK/US systems used by police, e.g. E-FIT, PRO-fit, FACES, Sketch) then match them to photos.

Experiment 2:

Aim: Photo array task to compare quality of external and internal composite features of first experiment (task intended to be similar to police line-up identification process).

Sample/participants: 48 undergraduate volunteers, Stirling University; 21 males, 27 females; aged 18–31 (mean age 21).

Method/procedure: Laboratory experiment (independent measures design). Participants tested individually; randomly assigned to one of four testing books (**easy** internal or external features; **hard** internal or external features). Task: view set of famous-face composites, then pick them out from photo line-up, comprising one celebrity and five distracter faces (foils).

Results:

Experiment 1: **Whole** and **external** composites sorted c. 33% correct, while **internal** composites only 19.5% correct (10% correct was expected by chance).

Experiment 2: Composites of **external** features were identified better (c. 42% correct) than **internal** features (c. 28% correct). Performance better on E-FITs (c. 40% correct identification) than PRO-fits (c. 30% correct).

Discussion: Wide age range means participants' familiarity with celebrities would vary. Expectation that greater familiarity would improve sorting; however, mean sorting scores did not change with familiarity for complete and internal features (only marginal differences for external).

Evaluation: Small samples not reliable. Atypical participants so cannot generalise findings. Good control/standardisation. Laboratory setting lacks ecological validity; however, photo array is similar to line-up procedure and witnesses often required to look at photos as part of identification process.

Debates: Very useful to inform police/courts about lack of reliability of witness identification. Psychology as science – standardisation/controls, meets criteria (replicability, falsifiability, objectivity).

Results:

Experiment 1: No significant difference found between conditions in accuracy of questionnaire responses overall, or on seven items relating to person B (although weapon condition slightly less accurate than control). Eye movement data: significant difference found with more eye fixations (with longer duration) in weapon condition than control. 'Line-up' data analysis: controls identification slightly more accurate than weapon condition (marginally significant).

Experiment 2: Questionnaire responses and line-up data analysis revealed weapon condition participants significantly less accurate than control (5% level).

Loftus, E.F. *et al.* (1987) Weapon focus

Background: Weapon focus refers to the concentration of a crime witness' attention on a weapon and the reduced ability to remember other crime details.

Aim: To investigate and assess evidence for weapon focus.

Experiment 1:

Sample/participants: 36 students, Washington University; aged 18–31.

Method/procedure: Laboratory experiment (independent measures design). Participants viewed a series of 18 slides (people in a queue for restaurant cashier). **Controls** saw 'person B' holding a cheque, while '**weapon**' condition saw

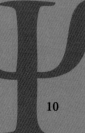

Fisher, R.P. *et al.* (1989) Field test of the cognitive interview technique (CIT)

Background/aim: To investigate the effectiveness of the CIT (in enhancing recall in victims and witnesses) in a field experiment.

Sample/participants: 16 experienced detectives from the Robbery Division, Florida Police Department (minimum of five years with robbery division).

Method/procedure: *Preliminary phase* (took *c.* four months to complete). Detectives tape-recorded interviews, using standard interviewing procedures. From amount of information gathered and recommendations of detectives' commanding officer, two groups formed: one trained in use of CIT (10); remainder untrained control group (6). Training conducted in four 1-hour group sessions, followed by tape-recorded, practice interview in the field (feedback received). *(Three in trained group did not complete full training programme due to changing schedules, court appearances, etc.)*

Post-training phase (took *c.* seven months to complete): seven trained and six controls tape-recorded 2–7 cases each, total of 47 interviews recorded (24 by trained, 23 by untrained/controls). As in preliminary phase, these interviews were mainly victims of commercial robbery/purse-snatching. Tape transcriptions and counting number of relevant, objective statements (e.g., physical descriptions of assailant, clothing, weapons, etc.) completed by two different groups of research assistants who were blind to condition of interviewer.

Results:

1.

▼ **Table 2.1** Mean number of facts elicited per interview by detectives

	Pre-training phase	**Post-training phase**
Trained	26.8	39.5
Untrained/controls	23.7	24.2

2. As a group the seven trained detectives elicited 47% more information after training compared to before training, with no loss of accuracy (improvement ranged from 34–115%) *(One detective did not improve; analysis of post-training interviews showed he did not use CIT recommended techniques.)*

Evaluation: Limitations means the results cannot be generalised – a) very small sample is unreliable; b) data based on restricted crime type; c) detectives experienced in robbery; d) geographically specific.
Debates: Nurture – techniques can be learned. Usefulness – CIT is effective in improving information retrieval from witnesses/victims; training is effective.

Extend/exam tip

Loftus & Mackworth (1978) people fixate more quickly, for longer and more often on unusual or highly informative objects (eye movements monitored by camera).

'person B' pulling a gun (both stimuli appeared in four slides). Eye movements recorded with a corneal reflection device. A 15-minute retention interval was followed by a 20-item, multiple-choice questionnaire (four response choices), including seven items about 'person B', e.g. 'What was the colour of B's coat?' Next, given a 'line-up' of 12 photos to test identification of 'person B'.

Experiment 2:

Sample/participants: 80 psychology students, Washington University (participating for extra credits).

Method/procedure: Laboratory experiment (independent measures design). 40 in **control** condition (cheque), 40 in **weapon** (gun) condition; same slide presentation as *experiment 1*. After 15-minute retention interval, participants given a seven-item multiple-choice test of items relating to 'person B', followed by 'line-up' identification test of 12 photos.

Conclusions: Findings provide support for weapon focus; however, authors speculate that similar results might be found with highly unusual objects.
Evaluation: Second study has more reliable sample size. Good control/standardisation means higher confidence in results. Lacks ecological validity (viewing slides), but could argue lack of stress (weapons condition) ethically sound.
Debates: Usefulness – has important implications for reliability of eyewitness identification and memory. Reductionist – does not take into account individual differences. Psychology as a science – standardisation/controls, recording of eye movements, etc., meets criteria of replicability, falsifiability and objectivity.

Mann, S. *et al.* (2004) Police officers' ability to detect lies

Background: Much research has been conducted on police officers' ability to detect deception whilst interviewing. A review by Vrij (2000) of studies conducted after 1980 identified accuracy rates of only *c.* 54% (50% would be achieved by chance). Vrij & Mann's (2001) study on 52 Netherlands police officers resulted in 94% (49/52) doing no better than chance (i.e. 50% accuracy) in detecting deception.

Aim: To investigate police officers' ability to distinguish truth and lies (during suspect interviews).

Sample/participants: 99 police officers working in Kent, UK (75 males, 24 females); mean age of *c.* 34. (78 detectives, 8 trainers, 4 traffic officers, 9 uniformed response officers.)

Method/procedure: Field experiment (using questionnaire and correlation). Participants first completed a questionnaire about their experience in detecting deception, then watched video clips (head and torso) of 14 suspects in real-life police interviews.
54 clips were used (ranging 6–145 seconds in length). Participants had to judge whether suspect was telling the truth or lying, then complete a scale on how confident they were about their judgements, then list what cues they had used which indicated suspect was lying.

Results:
1. Participants were *c.* 66% accurate in detecting *lies* and *c.* 64% accurate in detecting *truth* (NB. Wide-ranging individual differences) both significantly greater than chance level of 50%.
2. Correlations investigating relationship between experience in interviewing and accuracy in detecting a) truth and b) lies resulted in very weak positive correlations (0.20 and 0.18, at 5% level).
3. Cues used (and listed) by participants to detect lying were: gaze, movements, vagueness, contradictions (in accounts) and fidgeting.

Discussion: Levels of accuracy are higher than those found in previous studies. Interestingly police officers who were good at detecting lies rely more on story cues (e.g. contradictions) than commonly held belief that liars give themselves away by non-verbal cues (e.g. fidgeting or covering mouth with hand).

Evaluation: A serious limitation is the lack of a control group (to establish ordinary people's ability to detect deception), although ethical issues arise (see below).

Issues: Ethics: lay people cannot be exposed to sensitive material unless using actors/made up material (which results in lack of ecological validity and generalisability).

Debates: Suggestion that experience/training (nurture) can improve police officers' ability to detect deception which means this research is useful.

▲ **Figure 2.1**

Inbau, F. *et al.* (1986) Reid's 'Nine-steps' interrogation technique

The author is co-writer (with Reid) on a book entitled *Criminal Interrogation and Confessions*. Although a summary of the principles outlines a technique that clearly assumes the interviewee is guilty, Inbau *et al.* are opposed to the use of any interrogation technique that might result in the confession of an innocent person. An interview is considered the first appropriate course of action, which the authors recommend should be exploratory and non-accusatory. A clear distinction is made between interviewing and interrogating; where the former is considered to be an exploration and a fact-finding procedure, and the latter is recommended to take part later in the investigative process, when there is good reason to suspect guilt and the primary goal is to gather more information/ evidence about the crime committed and secure a confession. These are the (summarised) steps recommended:

Results: Coerced compliant type of confession (suspect confesses to escape/stop intolerable pressure of interrogation). Psychiatric examination: considered to be without mental illness. Psychometric tests:
1. IQ 94.
2. EPI (Eysenck's Personality Inventory): stable/extrovert.
3. Suggestibility scale (Gudjohnnson's): scored abnormally high (10).

Gudjohnnson, G.H. *et al.* (1990): A case of false confession

Background: The dangers of false confessions from suspects who are vulnerable, with mental health issues/learning difficulties or illiterate have previously been acknowledged. There is, however, a general assumption that an innocent person (without any of these difficulties) will not falsely confess.

Aim: To document a case of false confession.

Sample/participant: A 17-year-old, of average intelligence, with no mental health issues.

Method/procedure: Case study compiled from information summarised from several police interviews with the suspect and later psychiatric examination and psychometric tests of the suspect. Crime: murder, sexual assault and robbery of two elderly women found battered to death in their home and their savings missing. Interviewed by police: the first interview, in the presence of police officers only, lasted *c.* 14 hours, with some breaks. It included leading questions (see link below), accusations of lying and guilt, and suggestions/taunts about his sexual impotence. The second interview, conducted the next day, in the presence of the duty solicitor resulted in a retraction of the previous day's statement. Later, under pressure and following further accusations about his failure with women, he confessed.

Link: AS study, Loftus and Palmer.

Evaluation: Confrontational interrogations are more likely to lead to false confessions and the possibility of the real perpetrator not being found (and being at large to commit further crimes); public not protected; waste of time and resources.

Debates: Social determinism/situational explanations of behaviour. Useful – identifying that people other than those previously considered vulnerable to false confession is essential in order to ensure interview techniques produce valid confessions and to prevent miscarriages of justice.

Extend

1. Stephen Downing is an example of a coerced compliant type of false confession. He had a mental age of 11, learning difficulties and was convicted, aged 17, of rape/murder of a young woman. He served 27 years in prison and was denied earlier parole because he was classified as IDOM (in denial of murder).
2. Research: Henry Lee Lucas.

1. *Confront* the suspect with their supposed guilt concerning the offence.
2. Offer the suspect the opportunity to *shift blame* (onto another, or explaining, e.g. 'force of circumstances').
3. *Prevent*/interrupt the suspect if they attempt to *deny* guilt.
4. *Ignore denials*, i.e. suspect's explanations of how/why they could not have committed the offence.
5. Maintain good eye contact, use suspect's first name, 'understand'/acknowledge suspect's difficulties.
6. When suspect becomes quiet, *offer alternatives*.
7. Offer *two* alternative explanations of guilt.
8. Ensure *witnesses present* when suspect admits guilt.
9. Ensure confession is *written down* and *signed*.

Evaluation: This technique may result in false confessions when used with those who are vulnerable, young, highly suggestible and/or have some mental health issues/learning difficulties. Labelling someone as possibly guilty means subsequent behaviour may be interpreted in the light of that label

Links: AS Rosenhan study, e.g. denial of guilt is considered (psychodynamic perspective) as a (Freudian) defence of avoidance/denial of the truth; false confessions.

Debates: Social determinism/situational explanation of behaviour (i.e. admitting guilt/confessing).

OFFENDER PROFILING

Canter, D. *et al.* (2004): The organized/disorganized typology of serial murder: myth or model?

Background/aim: To investigate if there is empirical support (a scientific basis) for the organised/disorganised typology classification of serial killers (which originated from ad hoc interviews/case information on an unrepresentative, opportunity sample of 36 serial murderers who volunteered to talk to FBI agents, with no subsequent test on reliability and with known validity problems).

Sample/participants: 100 cases of serial, sexual homicides committed by 100 US serial killers (known as Missen Corpus data).

Method/procedure: Published Missen Corpus data cross-checked with court reports and, where possible, investigating officers. Content analysis (which identified 39 different crime 'factors') followed by multi-dimensional scaling test (SSA) of co-occurrence of 39 factors. Crimes followed Crime Classification Manual (CCM) in relation to crime scene and offender characteristics (third crime used).

▼ **Table 2.2** Examples of organised/disorganised crime scene variables/actions from Missen Corpus

Organised	Disorganised
Murder weapon missing 67%	Weapon left in victim 19%
Body concealed 58%	Body left in isolated spot 54%
Tampered with evidence 21%	Belongings scattered 47%

(100 cases – % indicates frequency of occurrence in this sample. Source: Canter et al., p. 305)

Results: Twice as many disorganised crime scene actions (26) were identified than organised (13). The frequency of actions/variables varies. Few examples found of co-occurring characteristics considered (previously) to indicate whether crime organised or disorganised. Smallest space analysis (SSA) used to test hypothesis of organised/disorganised typology (which would predict characteristics would fall into two distinct regions of SSA space) found that disorganised variables are scattered across the display with the organised variables mixed in among them. Ten variables (high-frequency/in central region of SSA display) that occur in more than 50% of cases are made up of equal numbers of organised and disorganised variables.

Conclusion: Analysis does not validate organised/disorganised typology.

Discussion: Canter proposes different styles of interaction (i.e. need to focus on offender's behaviour) with the victim (e.g. sexual control, mutilation) may be more useful in profiling.

Evaluation: The pre-established data base eliminates researcher bias (as does using the CCM), cross-checking of sources and statistical analysis means data generally considered robust/reliable.

Debates: Useful – statistical analysis eliminates researcher/interpretation bias. Psychology as science – Canter attempts to move the way offender profiling is conducted towards scientific procedures that can be checked for reliability, falsifiability and objectivity.

Results: Analysis of factors indicates that there are five variables that are central to rape (vaginal intercourse; no reaction to victim; impersonal language; surprise attack; victim's clothing disturbed), which Canter considers as indicative of an impersonal, surprise attack. Another constellation of variables – 'attempted intimacy' (e.g. offender requires victim to participate verbally and physically during assault, offender inquisitive about victim + four others); 'impersonal interaction' (e.g. blitz attack, impersonal language, no response to victim's reactions + three others) would be predicted to be a reflection of a general approach to women in offender's everyday life (seeing them as sex objects, rather than as people).

Canter, D. (1996) A multivariate model of sexual offence behaviour

Aim: To identify associations between aspects of the offender's characteristics and offence behaviour using scientific, objective measures.

Sample/participants: 27 sex offenders (and their 66 sexual offences documented by various English police forces, involving sexual assaults against strangers).

Method/procedure: Initial exploration of a range of crimes on which full information was available. Thirty-three offence variables were identified through data available (e.g. victim statements and police reports, not collected for research purposes

Canter, D. (1995) The case of John Duffy

Background: Canter became involved in this case in 1985 when the police (convinced that a series of rapes/murders were the acts of one man) asked if he could help catch the man 'before he kills again' (Gross, 2010). Material was later documented in Canter's *Criminal Shadows* book.

Aim: To systematically document crimes, crime scene details, chronology (and subsequently geography) in order to infer possible behavioural characteristics of an offender, using psychological principles/knowledge and scientific methods. Canter calls this Investigative Psychology and believes: 1. Crime involves communication between two people. The way the offender behaves towards victim will reveal something about the offender's dealing with people in everyday life. 2. A systematic/scientific approach is essential, which includes consideration of all available evidence (nothing should be discounted just because it 'doesn't fit'). 3. An offender is likely to commit crime, at least initially, in a familiar area (often called a 'home' range) – this may be where the offender lives/works. Geographical mapping (and timings) of crime can help identify this range.

Method/procedure: Systematic data evaluation exercise in order to generate an offender profile. Data obtained from police databases. It is not a case study in the usual psychological research sense.

Results: Canter's profile suggested a number of possible offender characteristics which allowed the police to narrow down their list of c. 2000 suspects (linked to the crimes by blood group). Duffy was originally 1505th (Harrower, 2001). Duffy was apprehended and ultimately convicted in 1988 of two murders and five rapes.

▼ **Table 2.3** Extract of David Canter's profile of John Duffy

Profile of likely offender	Details matched
Lives in Kilburn/Cricklewood area where first three offences occurred	Duffy lived in Kilburn
Need to dominate women	Duffy was violent and had previously attacked his wife
Keeps souvenirs from crimes	Duffy had 33 door keys, each taken from victim as souvenir

(Adapted from source: Harrower, J. (2001) Crime – Psychology in Practice, pp. 56–7. London: Hodder Arnold.)

Debates: Individual explanations of behaviour. Very useful – identifying possible characteristics of an offender allows police to narrow down their list of suspects, direct their resources and ultimately apprehend the offender more quickly. (NB. It does NOT allow the identification of a particular individual.)

Exam tip

Be able to describe and evaluate British (bottom-up) and the American (top-down) approaches to offender profiling.

so no detailed protocol or training for data collection). Behavioural variables with low frequencies were excluded (considered of less value here in developing general principles). Variables categorised with yes/no values (i.e. presence or absence of behaviour). Content analysis and subsequent Smallest Space Analysis (SSA) (a multi-dimensional scaling procedure examining relationship between one variable and every other examined, which represents correlation between variables as distances in statistically derived geometric space).

Evaluation: Taking a statistical approach to data analysis allows greater confidence in results, subjective interpretation is eliminated and the findings can be considered more reliable. Small sample (although fairly large number of offences) and restricted crime type.

Debates: Useful – as statistical analysis can be done on different crime types. Less reductionist as large number of variables/behaviour investigated. Psychology as science – see Debates for the Canter *et al.* (2004) study, p.14.

PERSUADING A JURY

Pennington, N. and Hastie, R. (1998) Effects of evidence order on verdicts

Background: Previous research on primacy and recency effects cannot be applied to the courtroom and to the possible advantage/disadvantage to defence/prosecution because of conflicting findings.

Aim: To investigate the effect of story order and jurors' confidence on jurors' verdicts.

Sample/participants: 130 (paid) students at Northwestern and Chicago Universities, USA.

Method/procedure: Laboratory experiment with independent measures design. Participants allocated roughly equally to one of four conditions (see Table 3.1): hearing 39 prosecution items (i.e. 'guilty' evidence) in 1. story order or 2. witness order; hearing 39 defence items (i.e. 'not guilty' evidence) in 3. story order or 4. witness order.

▼ **Table 3.1** Independent measures design to test effects of evidence order on verdicts

Four conditions	
39 *prosecution* items in *story* order	39 *defence* items in *story* order
39 *prosecution* items in *witness* order	39 *defence* items in *witness* order

Participants first listened to a tape recording of a stimulus trial (which had been edited/adapted from a real-life case to follow evidence items according to condition assigned), then responded to a questionnaire where they were asked to give a verdict (guilty/not guilty) and rate confidence in their decision on 5-point scale.

Results: Story order resulted in 59% guilty verdicts compared to 31% in witness order (for prosecution items) and 78% guilty verdicts compared to 63% in witness order (for defence items). Greatest confidence was expressed by those who heard evidence in story order (either defence or prosecution).

Evaluation: Controlled for primacy and recency effects, therefore reliable and higher confidence in results (and see general evaluation).

Debates: Usefulness – essential to ensure that courtroom procedures do not advantage/disadvantage either prosecution/defence counsel and thereby pervert the course of justice.

Conclusions: Expert testimony improved jurors' knowledge and in some form reduced jurors' reliance on witness confidence (e.g. jurors paid more attention to evidence). Where no expert witness testimony was given, witness confidence effected jurors' judgements.

Debates: (see general evaluation)

Cutler, B.L. *et al.* (1989) The effects of expert witness testimony on jurors' decisions

Background: There is concern from previous research about jurors' over-reliance on eyewitness testimony, which calls into question their scrutiny of evidence.

Aim: To investigate the effects of expert testimony (which casts doubt on the accuracy of eyewitness testimony) on jurors' judgements.

Sample/participants: 538 introductory psychology undergraduates, given extra course credits, USA.

Method/procedure: A laboratory experiment. A videotape of a mock, armed-robbery trial (following format of actual trial) was viewed by participants in small groups (2–8 participants), who then independently completed a questionnaire on dependent measures, memory test and rating scales. IVs: 1. Witness identifying conditions (WIC) either **poor** (robber disguised, brandishing handgun, 14-day delay in witness identification) or **good** (robber not disguised, handgun hidden, 2-day delay in witness identification). 2. Witness confidence either **high** (testified 100% confident in correct identification) or **low** (testified 80% confident). 3. Expert witness (psychologist) testimony: either descriptive only or descriptive + quantified (or no expert witness). 4. Expert witness opinion on accuracy of identification (rating scale, 0–25, where 0 = least likely to be correct): either low (7 in poor WIC trials), or high (20 in good WIC trials), or no expert witness. DVs: 1. verdicts (guilty/not guilty); 2. memory test; 3. juror knowledge; 4. rating on probability that a) defendant guilty; b) eye witness identification correct.

Pickel, K.L. (1995) The effects of inadmissible evidence on jurors' verdicts

Background: Judges may rule evidence/testimony as inadmissible if it is believed that jurors may be unduly influenced by it, but previous research has sometimes shown that instructions to disregard evidence makes it more salient (known as reactance theory).

Aim: To investigate whether evidence ruled inadmissible by a judge influences jurors' verdicts, whether the credibility of a witness affects jurors' ability to disregard inadmissible testimony from that witness and whether the 'fairness' of evidence influenced jurors' verdicts.

Method: A series of three laboratory experiments using independent measures designs, where participants were randomly allocated to conditions.

Experiment 1

Sample/participants: 236 psychology students at Ball State University (volunteered in partial fulfilment of course requirement)

Method/procedure: Prior conviction evidence (eight different versions of an audiotape). IVs: 1. Evidence of prior conviction (four conditions): a) admissible, b) inadmissible without explanation, c) inadmissible with explanation and d) control (critical evidence not presented). 2. Credibility of witness (two conditions): a) high credibility, b) low credibility. DVs: 1. verdicts (guilty/not guilty). 2. Estimate of probability of defendant's guilt. 3. Rating (10-point scale) of extent to which evidence of prior conviction caused belief in defendant's guilt. 4. Rating (7-point scale) on credibility of witness. Participants first listened to an audiotape of a fictional trial involving theft.

Results: The highest percentage of guilty verdicts were given in the evidence ruled admissible condition and the lowest given in control and inadmissible without explanation conditions. Significant difference (5% level) between guilty verdicts when witness credibility high (58%), compared to low (44%).

Experiment 2

Sample/participants: 290 psychology students at Ball State University (volunteered in partial fulfilment of course requirement)

Method/procedure: Hearsay evidence followed a method/procedure similar to *Experiment 1* except hearsay evidence presented (where witness reported hearing someone else say the defendant had said something incriminating).

Results: A higher percentage of participants in the admissible evidence condition (than control) gave guilty verdicts (significant at 5% level). Probability of guilt ratings was higher when witness credibility was high.

Experiment 3

Sample/participants: 121 psychology students at Ball State University (volunteers)

Method/procedure: Hypothesised that 'hearsay' would be considered less fair than prior conviction evidence.

Results: The results supported the hypothesis: hearsay evidence received a lower fairness rating.

Evaluation (general – all three research studies): Mock trial evidence, mock jurors and laboratory settings means all these studies lack ecological validity; we do not know if jurors would make the same decisions in real life (here decisions have **no** consequences); cannot apply/ generalise findings. Large, reliable samples, but geographically-specific and students are atypical/ unrepresentative.

Debates: Situational explanation of behaviour/social determinism (courtroom procedures) are not very useful, based on evaluation above but very useful to identify any courtroom procedures which could adversely affect the course of justice. Psychology as science – high levels of control/ standardisation, statistical analysis means research meets criteria for replicability, objectivity and falisfiability.

Results: (Extensive statistical analysis).
1. When WIC good, a higher percentage of guilty verdicts given (effect increased where expert witness had given descriptive testimony). Jurors' memory was tested to rule out poor memory as a possible confounding variable (85% correctly recalled testimony).
2. Ratings of credibility of witness varied with witness confidence levels: witness rated more credible when she testified 100% confident in identification.
3. Jurors had greater confidence in the accuracy of the witness identification when WIC were good (with a stronger effect with witness testifying 100% confident).
4. Correlation between verdict and jurors' perceived probability that identification was correct = 0.66.

WITNESS APPEAL

Castellow, W.A. *et al.* (1990) The effects of physical attractiveness on jury verdicts

Background: Research has confirmed that physically attractive defendants are treated more leniently by mock jurors than unattractive defendants. The 'halo' effect and Dion's (1972) 'what is beautiful is good' also suggest we are biased towards perceiving attractive individuals in a positive way.

Aim: To investigate 1. whether an attractive defendant is less likely to be found guilty than an unattractive defendant and 2. whether an attractive witness means a defendant is more likely to be found guilty.

Sample/participants: 71 male and 74 female undergraduates on an introductory psychology course (participating for extra credits) at East Carolina University, USA.

Method/procedure: A laboratory experiment using an independent measures design, in a mock trial format, based on a sexual harassment case (constructed by researchers, based on two real cases). Participants read the case, which was accompanied by photos of both defendant and plaintive. Photos used had been rated independently by a large sample on a 9-point scale and the lowest (least attractive) and highest (most attractive) scoring photos were selected. IVs: 1. gender of participant; 2. defendant's attractiveness; 3. plaintiff's attractiveness. Main DV was participants' verdicts (i.e. guilty/not guilty); also asked to rate defendant and plaintiff on 11-point bi-polar adjective scales (e.g. dull–exciting, insincere–sincere).

Results:
1. Attractive defendants were given fewer guilty verdicts (71%) than unattractive (83%) with an attractive plaintiff, and 41% compared to 69% guilty verdicts with an unattractive plaintiff.
2. On 11 measures of personal characteristics, both males and females rated the attractive defendant more positively than the unattractive defendant on *all* variables.

Evaluation: Independent rating of photos eliminates researcher bias.
Debates: Determinism (social) of attractiveness. Ethnocentrism – attractiveness will vary with cultural ideals. Usefulness – see general evaluation, **not** very useful; however, essential to identify factors which might bias jurors and possibly lead to miscarriages of justice.

Results: Percentage of guilty verdicts for disguise and weapon focus resulted in c. 63–64% whether high or low (i.e. *not* significant; neither were the other seven variables). Witness confidence (about identification) was the only statistically significant result with 100% confidence expressed by witness resulting in 67% guilty verdicts, compared to 60% guilty verdicts given when 80% confidence expressed by witness.

Penrod, S. and Cutler, B. (1995) The effect of witness confidence on jurors' assessment of eyewitness evidence

Background: Jurors seem to be highly influenced by witness confidence, perhaps believing that a confident witness is more likely to be accurate/reliable.

Aim: To identify juror sensitivity to witness confidence and other factors.

Sample/participants: Undergraduates and eligible and experienced jurors.

Method/procedure: Participants watched a videotape. Ten variables (IVs) were manipulated (with 'high' and 'low' conditions) e.g. disguise ('high': suspect heavily disguised; 'low': suspect minimally disguised); weapon focus ('high': weapon clearly brandished; 'low': weapon visible); witness confidence ('high': expressed 100% confidence in identification; 'low' expressed 80% confidence). DVs: jurors' verdicts.

Results:

1. No significant differences in guilty verdicts were found between the three conditions; however, females gave more guilty verdicts, c. 59%, than males, c. 39%.

2. No significant differences in the three conditions regarding the jury's perception of the defendant's credibility, but females rated the defendant *less* credible than males (consistent with their guilty verdicts).

3. There were no significant differences found across the three conditions regarding the credibility of the witness; however, female students rated the child as *more* credible (consistent with their guilty verdicts).

A second experiment, using 60 student participants, followed essentially the same procedures, although in addition it manipulated warnings given to the jury about the use of shields/videotapes. The film was stopped and measures were taken *after* the child had given evidence; this is not the procedure followed in a real courtroom.

Ross, D. *et al.* (1994) The impact of protective shields/videotaped testimony on conviction rates

Background: Protective devices for child eyewitnesses are used to reduce psychological stress: however, there is concern about whether their use is prejudicial i.e. implies guilt (credibility deflation) of defendant /believability of witness (credibility inflation).

Aim: 1. To investigate the impact of protective shields/videotaped evidence on guilty verdicts. 2. To investigate if protective devices result in credibility inflation or deflation.

Sample/participants: 300 introductory psychology class college students (gender balanced); the majority were white and middle class.

Method/procedure: A laboratory experiment using an independent measures design. Participants assigned equally to three conditions **(IVs)**: Child testimony given in 1) open court (in full view); 2) behind (4 x 6 ft) screen; 3) via video-link. Participants watched (one of three versions) of a 2-hour, trial simulation based on a real case, filmed by a professional crew in a real courtroom, with actors role-playing a child sexual abuse case. **DVs:** 1. Verdicts (guilty/not guilty); 2. Credibility rating of defendant; and 3. Credibility rating of witness. Two real attorneys gave advice to ensure trial was ecologically valid in terms of legal procedure.

Evaluation (general – all three studies): Large samples are more reliable, although student samples are atypical/unrepresentative. Mock trials and laboratory experiments, where decisions have no consequences, are low in ecological validity and therefore we have to be very careful in applying/generalising the findings.
Debates: No evidence of social determinism/situational explanations of behaviour from these courtroom procedures. Usefulness – from evaluation above, not very useful; however, to ensure no miscarriages of justice it is very useful to know courtroom procedures do not bias the judicial process.

▲ Figure 3.1

Additional: In nine other studies reported here, testing the relationship between identification accuracy and pre-identification confidence in ability to make an identification, the confidence – accuracy correlation ranged from 0.00 to 0.20, i.e. no correlation – very weak correlation. In other words, confidence in ability is not related to accuracy in identification.
Evaluation: The use of eligible and experienced jurors as part of the sample strengthens reliability only marginally.
Debates: Determinism (social) witness confidence. Usefulness – it is imperative that jurors critically examine all evidence and are not swayed by witness confidence, to prevent miscarriages of justice.

Extend

Penrod & Cutler include an extensive review of other work, e.g. how well briefed witnesses are affects perceptions of confidence (and witness performance) and the malleability of confidence levels in eye witnesses.

REACHING A VERDICT

Hastie, R. *et al.* (1983) Stages in decision-making and influences

Background: In England the legal system engages 12 jurors who are directed to reach a unanimous verdict or, if that isn't achievable, a majority decision by 10 of 12 jurors. As jury decision-making cannot be directly studied, the authors are applying findings from social psychological research into groups and decision-making to the jury process.

Aim: To offer a model of the stages of jury decision-making:

Model: 1. **Orientation period:** which may start with agenda setting followed by open discussion, when questions are posed/discussed and facts of the case explored and where different opinions arise.
2. **Open confrontation:** likely to be characterised by debate and challenge, in-depth focus/exploration of details, consideration of alternative views/different interpretations, pressure on the minority to agree with majority becomes more overt, establishing support for the group (majority) decision.
3. **Reconciliation:** group consensus is reached following resolution of conflicts and easing of tensions.

Evaluation: Applying findings from research which has not specifically studied the jury deliberation process may not be reliable; however, the fact that there are strong parallels with Tuckman's theory of group formation, which has been well received/used (link: Sport) means some reliability may be inferred.

Debates: Situational explanations/social determinism (e.g. being locked in a room; the need to reach a unanimous verdict). Reductionist – ignores individual/personality factors which are likely to impact on decision making. Usefulness – (see above comments on Tuckman) can be considered as quite useful.

Asch, S.E. (1955) The power of influence and conformity

Background/aim: To investigate the effect of majority influence on a minority (of one) using a simple perceptual discrimination task.

Sample/participants: 123 male students (from three different institutions), USA.

Method/procedure: A laboratory experiment (also used interviews). A series of trials were run with groups of 7–9 students. Participants were seated at a table; they viewed two cards – on one was the 'standard' (a single vertical line); on the other were three vertical lines of varying length, one of which was same length as 'standard'; participants had to choose which of three lines was same as the 'standard', see figure 3.2. In each group one was true/real (naïve) participant, others were confederates. Procedure engineered so that true/real participant always gave response last. Confederates were briefed to give the same incorrect answer on certain trials. There were 18 trials in each series and on 12 the majority/confederates responded incorrectly, although instructed to answer correctly on the first two trials. Participants were interviewed at the end to identify reasons for conformity.

Variations on experiment: 1. Varying the number of participants seated around table, from one confederate + one real participant to 16 (i.e. 15 confederates). 2. Having a single dissenter who responded *correctly* before real participant answered. 3. Having a single dissenter who responded *incorrectly* before real participant answered.

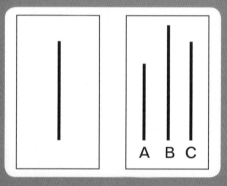

▲ **Figure 3.2** Asch's line discrimination task – which line (A, B or C) is the same length as the line on the left?

Results:
1. Conformity/agreement with majority (i.e. an incorrect answer) was given in c. 36.8% of trials, although there was variation in conformity (i.e. individual differences): 25% of participants *never* agreed with majority while some individuals went with majority nearly all the time.
2. Interview data varied from participants believing they were wrong (or deficient) and the majority were correct, to some participants reporting they did not want to 'spoil results'. All yielding/conforming participants underestimated the frequency of their conformity.
3. Variation results: when real participant was one of two, they invariably did *not* conform. Conformity rose to 13.6% of trials with two confederates and to 31.8% with three confederates. Beyond this number, the conformity rate remained steady, regardless of size. 'Dissenter' trials resulted in conformity reducing to c. 5%.

Nemeth, C. and Wachtler, J. (1974) Minority influence and perceived autonomy in decision-making

Background: A classic experiment by Moscovici (1985) involving colour perception judgements concluded that consistency and lack of compromise are essential for minority influence to be exerted.

Aim: To investigate the role of perceived autonomy on minority influence.

Sample/participants: 116 male (paid $1.50) volunteers at Northwestern University, USA.

Method/procedure: Participants were given an injury/compensation case study to read (in which plaintiff was suing for $25,000). They then had to write down an amount of compensation they would award before being conducted, in groups of five, to a discussion room. Participants either chose or were assigned a chair (either head of table or side seat).
A control group was used. One confederate was used on all trials (trained for 25 hours in verbal/non-verbal behaviour and 'blind' to experimental hypothesis). He adopted a 'minority' position (i.e. argued compensation of $3,000). Groups instructed to reach a unanimous decision in 40 minutes (for which an extra 50c would be paid). Afterwards, participants completed a questionnaire asking if opinion about compensation amount and attitudes had changed, and about their perceptions of other group participants.

Results: No groups reached consensus in 40 minutes. Initial compensation mean was $14,670. When confederate chose head seat, he exerted influence (i.e. compensation reduced to a mean of $10,375). **Chosen head** condition more effective (as measured by lowered compensation 'awards') than the **assigned head** condition (5% significance level).

Questionnaire data: Confederate perceived as more consistent, more independent, more of a leader and more confident (1% significance) than other participants. Also reported that confederate made them think/assess their own positions more. Confederate perceived as more consistent and more of a leader when he occupied the head seat than when he occupied a side seat.

Evaluation: Controls (e.g. training confederate, 'blind' to hypothesis; control group) allows for greater confidence in results/data more reliable.
Debates: Social determinism/situational explanations of behaviour (choosing head seat). Usefulness – would seem to suggest it is essential to have a round table (no head seat) to prevent undue influence.

Evaluation: Laboratory experiments lack ecological validity and care should be taken when applying/generalising the findings. All-male sample is gender biased and findings cannot be generalised. Interviewing obtained important (valid) data about explanations of behaviour.
Debates: Situational explanations of behaviour/social determinism, however, 'resisting' conformity indicates free will. Usefulness – this has implications for education/training.

Extend/exam tip

All research is reductionist, however, it is important to acknowledge other factors which are liable to affect jury decision-making to obtain good marks. For example, personality factors (e.g. high/low self-esteem and confidence), age, gender, education, prior attitudes, religious/cultural/spiritual beliefs and previous experiences.

Gillis, C.A. and Nafekh, M. (2005) The effects of community-based employment on re-offending

Background: Previous research has confirmed lack of employment prospects/unemployment as serious risk factors for re-offending. A Prison Reform Trust (2007) report highlights that a typical adult offender has poor literacy and numeracy skills and has left school with no qualifications.

Aim: To explore the impact of employment on re-offending (recidivism) with offenders on conditional release.

Sample/participants: Started with a data base of *c.* 23,500, 95% male (*c.* 22,300) and 5% female (*c.* 1,200) on conditional release (prior to end of sentence) between January 1998 and January 2005. After matching the sample (see below) was 4640 male, 156 female.

Method/procedure: Content analysis of Correctional Service of Canada's database, followed by statistical analysis using matched pairs (matched on gender, risk level, release year, sentence length, etc.). Matched sample divided into two groups: i) employed upon release; ii) not employed.

Data analysed to draw comparisons between groups on: 1. Return to custody before end of sentence; 2. Return to custody with a new offence before end of sentence; and 3. Return to custody without a new offence before end of sentence.

Results:
1. From date of conditional release men take an average (median) of *c.* six months to find employment while women take *c.* ten months.
2. Men: employed more likely to remain on conditional release until the end of their sentence than unemployed. The median time to return to custody was also later for the employed group (37 months, compared to 11 months for unemployed). Employed men were also less likely to return to custody with a new offence or technical revocation (e.g. breach of parole conditions).
3. Women: employed more likely to remain on conditional release until the end of their sentence (than unemployed); 70% of employed women remained on conditional release compared to *c.* 55% of unemployed. Similarly the employed women were less likely to return with a new offence than unemployed.

Evaluation: Use of PDP files (includes large number of factors) attempts to be less reductionist. Researcher bias is eliminated by use of data gathered by others; however, cannot evaluate how systematically/objectively data was collated.
Debates: Useful (as less reductionist) and highlights 'time of suicide' risk, although reducing risks likely to be curtailed due to financial/resource limitations. Social determinism/situational explanations of behaviour (prison situation).

Evaluation: Using an official database and statistical analysis eliminates researcher bias; the large sample is reliable; geographically specific, cannot necessarily generalise findings.
Debates: Social determinism/situational explanations of behaviour (employment schemes reduce recidivism) and also very useful.

Dooley, E. (1990) Prison suicide in England and Wales

Background: The rise of unnatural deaths in prisons (which is disproportionate to increases in the prison population), particularly suicides, are of great concern, as is the increase in self-harm. The risk factors encompass those that are both individual and institutional/situational (e.g. mental illness, history of psychiatric disorder, history of self-harm, substance abuse, losses (of social contact, relationships), victimisation by other inmates, difficulties in coping with the prison regime, guilt).

Aim: Investigating unnatural deaths by suicide occurring in prisons in England and Wales between 1972 and 1987.

Data: Of 442 unnatural deaths recorded, 300 given a verdict of suicide; 52 a verdict of consciously self-inflicted injury (CSI), the remaining a variety of verdicts. 295 suicides (98.3% of total) were studied, 290 male, 5 female (age range 15–79).

Method/procedure: Content analysis of Prison Department Personal (PDP) files (containing information on inmate's background, previous offences, time spent in custody, accounts/statements from prison staff/inmates on circumstances surrounding the death, coroner's inquest, admission details, difficulties encountered – personal or prison). Extensive statistical analysis conducted.

Haney, C. and Zimbardo, P. (1998) USA prison policy: the past and future

Background: The Stanford Prison Experiment (SPE) conducted in 1973 and Reicher & Haslam (2006) BBC prison study gives some indication as to the psychological distress of incarceration.

Aim: 1. To review the past 25 years' of USA prison policy: a) 'The criminal justice systems has become increasingly harsh and punitive' (p. 712), i.e. the concept of rehabilitation had been discredited. b) Many US states changed to determinate sentencing (i.e. removal of the possibility of parole/being let out for good behaviour). c) Building of new prisons to cope with increase in prison population. d) USA had more people in prison than any other modern (i.e. western, industrialised) nation. e) Racial bias identified. African–American men make up *c.* 48% of prison population, although only comprise 6% of general population. Women and Hispanics also over-represented compared to white men. f) Drug offenders over-represented (64% of black male defendants and 71% of black female defendants convicted in drugs trials). g) Increase in the special security facilities where offenders live in extreme isolation (e.g. locked up 23/24 hours); many US prisons are unable to carry out training, education, counselling and treatment programmes.

Aim: 2. To suggest improvements to the prison system: a) The negative psychological effects of prison are well documented (link – AS Reicher and Haslam study) and should be evaluated, monitored and 'treated'. b) Prisons are over-crowded and contain mentally unstable inmates; threats of violence are commonplace. Prison sentencing should be used sparingly/serious alternatives should be considered. c) Transitional/decompression programmes needed to bridge the gap between the extremes of prison regimes and release. d) Assessments/psychometric tests are insufficiently sensitive to be predictive in a prison environment. e) Change is best from 'without' i.e. independent of prison system. f) Psychological knowledge/research (almost been completely disregarded) should inform policy/changes.

Extend/exam tip
1. What is the purpose of prisons? To rehabilitate? To punish? 'Prisons don't work' argument assumes the purpose is a deterrent/preventative.
2. Farrington et al. (2002) investigates the effects of intensive regimes on young male offenders' recidivism rates.
3. Grendon Underwood whose running is based on psychological principles has had lower re-offending rates.

Debates: Social determinism/situational explanations of behaviour. Not very useful as US legal system and culture different to UK (ethnocentric to apply findings).

Results: Analysis of suicides: 90% (266/295) were by hanging; 3.7% (11/195) from drug overdose/poisoning; 33% (97) had a history of psychiatric contact; 27% (80) had past record of alcohol abuse; 23% (69) of drug abuse; 43% (126) had on record deliberate self-injury in the past. 47% (139/295) of suicides while prisoners on remand. 50% of suicides were between midnight and 8 a.m.

▼ **Table 4.1** Attributed motivation for suicide in prison

	No.	%
Prison situation	118	40.0
Mental disorder	66	22.4
Outside pressures	45	15.3
Guilt for offence	37	12.5
Not known	29	9.8

(Source: Adapted from Dooley (1990))

▲ **Figure 4.1**

ALTERNATIVES TO IMPRISONMENT

Mair, G. and May, C. (1997) Experiences of offenders on probation orders

Background: Probation services have been under increasing pressure to demonstrate their effectiveness. One measure used has been reconviction (recidivism) rates.

Aim: To investigate offenders' experiences of probation orders.

Sample/participants: 1213 (82% male, 18% female); c. 50% age range 16–24; 93% white; c. 20% were employed/self-employed. First time on probation for c. 50%. Recruited from 22/55 probation areas (England and Wales).

Method/procedure: Random sampling of Home Office Probation Index database. Of 3299 offenders, c. 40% not contactable (e.g. taken into custody; probation order terminated; moved), leaving 1986. With a 61% response rate (8% refusal rate) 1213 were interviewed for c. one hour, mainly at probation offices (1994). Questions covered offender's background, offending history, drug/alcohol use in last 12 months and probation experience. Pilot study conducted before drafting questionnaire.

Results: 47% reported probation order was extremely useful. 62% reported that they thought the probation officer would help sort out problems. 45% reported that they thought being on a probation order was helping them keep out of trouble. 37% reported they thought the probation order would stop them re-offending. Self-reports of drug use: cannabis used by 57% of male (aged 16–29) in last 12 months (compared to 25% of this age group in general population). About 40% of offenders reported a convicted family* member (c. 33% mentioned a parent) and c. 75% reported having friends** who had been in trouble with the law.

Evaluation: Sample is atypical/unrepresentative (many would not take part/were not contactable/did not turn up for their appointment); care needed in generalising/applying findings. Socially desirable responses/lying possible (question validity). Effectiveness of probation order would be better assessed by matching participants for age, gender, crime type with offenders **not** on probation orders and comparing re-offending rates. (Link: **Turning to Crime**, Farrington et al.* and Sutherland**.) **Debates:** Situational explanation of behaviour/social determinism (of probation orders). Usefulness – questionable given validity problems, the unrepresentative sample and no comparison group.

Sherman, L.W. and Strang, H. (2007) Restorative justice and re-offending prevention

Background: Restorative justice (RJ) is most usually victim-offender mediation (conducted with a police officer trained in RJ programme). It can also involve restitution/reparation payments ordered by the courts. Two-fold purpose: to get offender to face up to consequences of their crime/take responsibility; to allow victim the opportunity to confront the offender.

Aim: To review RJ programmes and reach conclusions about effectiveness (particularly in relation to re-offending).

Method/procedure: An international review/literature search (limited to studies written in English) was conducted using online databases/ library catalogues, existing published reviews on RJ effectiveness, publication bibliographies and referrals by experts in the field.

Results: 1. RJ reduced recidivism (re-offending) *more than prison* with adults and *as well as prison* with youths – from six rigorous field tests involving violent crime, three with randomised controlled trials (under 30 year olds, Canberra; under 18 females, Northumbria; mainly male, under 14s, Indianapolis). Effects also confirmed for adult males, West Yorkshire and West Midlands; violent families in Canada. Substantial reductions in re-offending (violence and property crime) found in a Canadian study (138 offenders, compared to a matched sample who served their sentence in prison); RJ two-year conviction rates were 11% compared to 37%. 2. RJ works better with crimes involving personal victims. 3. Victim effects: benefits predominantly from victim-offender mediation (evidence less clear about financial reparation); based on willing victims; short-term benefits are improved mental health. Two London studies found reduced post-traumatic stress (long-term benefits could be reduced health risks, e.g. heart disease). 4. RJ provided both victims and offenders with more satisfaction (four studies reported victims prefer RJ compared to usual court justice). 5. RJ reduced victims' desire for violent revenge against their offenders (found in four studies).
Additional result (alternative source): Reduced costs of criminal justice when used instead of court case (Harrower, 2001: Northumbrian study, cost of RJ £720 per case, re-offending rate 35%, compared with cost of court case £2,500, re-offending rate 67%.)

Results: *Phase 1: Black defendant/White victim:* Statistical analysis involving low/high Black stereotypicality and six non-racial factors known to influence sentencing (e.g. severity of murder, defendant's attractiveness) found that (above and beyond the co-variates) the more stereotypically Black defendants were more likely to receive a death sentence than defendants whose appearance was perceived as less stereotypically Black (5% significance).

Phase 2: Black defendant/Black victim: Death sentencing rate was 27%, compared to 41% of cases involving White victim. Same statistical analyses found that perceived stereotypicality of Black defendants, convicted of murdering a Black victim, did *not* predict death sentencing.

Eberhardt, J.L. *et al.* (2006) Stereotypically black features and likelihood of receiving the death sentence

Background: Numerous research studies have found that murderers of white victims are more likely than murderers of black victims to be sentenced to death.

Aim: To investigate whether the probability of receiving the death penalty is significantly influenced by the degree to which the defendant is perceived to have a stereotypically Black appearance (e.g. broad nose, thick lips, dark skin).

Phase 1: Black defendant/white victim:

Database: 44 (of 600+) death-eligible (Philadelphia) cases involving Black male defendants convicted of murdering White victims from 1979–1999.

Method/procedure: Standardised, black and white photos of defendants were presented (slide-show, randomised presentation order) to two groups of naïve (Stanford undergraduate) raters (who did not know photos were of convicted murderers and 'blind' to purpose of study); photos rated on how stereotypically Black they appeared (11-point rating scale). Data analysed for effects of order and raters' race, but none found.

Group 1 raters: 32 (26 White, 4 Asian, 2 other ethnicities); Group 2 raters: 19 (6 White, 11 Asian, 2 other ethnicities).

Phase 2: Black defendant/black victim:

Using same database/procedures described above, 308 cases identified involving Black male defendant convicted of murdering Black victims and 118 obtained by random sampling.

Evaluation: Controls/standardisation means we can have greater confidence in findings/more reliable. Sample sizes of death-eligible cases fairly (White victim) and very (Black victim) reliable.

Debates: Social/biological determinism/ nature (skin colour/race), also nurture (learned attitudes/beliefs/stereotypes). Very useful to eliminate bias in the judicial process which aims to be fair, regardless of race (age, creed, etc.).

Evaluation: Authors followed protocols for assessing evidence which eliminates researcher/interpretation bias and conclusions considered more reliable. Sample sizes were usually large, although they ranged from 14–465 (violent crime mean sample size *c.* 140; property crime mean sample size *c.* 180).

Debates: Social determinism/situational explanation of behaviour (RJ programme). **Usefulness** – limited by crime type/willingness of victim; however, research would support the application of RJ programmes more widely.

Extend
Eberhardt et al. (2004) found participants associated black physical traits with criminality.

TREATMENT PROGRAMMES

Cann, J. (2006) The impact of cognitive skills programmes on reconviction/recidivism

Background: Cognitive skills programmes were introduced into HM Prison Service (England and Wales) in the early 1990s. Rationale: criminal behaviour is a result of 'faulty thinking'; challenging this will reduce re-offending.

Aim: To assess the effectiveness (based on reconviction rates) of cognitive skills programmes.

Sample/participants: 180 females started either the Enhanced Thinking Skills (ETS) programme (114) or Reasoning and Rehabilitation (R&R) (66), compared to 540 female offenders (controls) who did *not* participate in such programmes.

Method/procedure: ETS and R&R delivered to female offenders in custody. Controls matched retrospectively (ethnicity, offence type, year of discharge, expected reconviction rate based on revised OGRS2). Programmes aimed at medium-high risk offenders, although less than one-third of women so categorised. Programmes should comprise 36 sessions of 2.5 hours each; participants have to complete 'homework' in-between sessions and after the course ends. *(NB. Participants did **not** receive full programme and delivery was inconsistent. 14 participants (8%) did not complete the programme.)*

Results: No statistically significant differences between programme participants and controls on one- and two-year reconviction rates; either overall or within risk category comparisons – low/high risk. Evidence of effectiveness of programme not established.

(NB. Evaluation of cognitive skills programmes with male adults and young offenders (Cann et al. 2003) found R&R had no statistically significant impact on reconviction, while ETS programme completers had statistically significant lower reconviction rates. R&R was withdrawn from use in 2004.)

Evaluation: Unsound to make any conclusions about effectiveness of programme when it was not delivered/completed; not designed for women; used with mostly low-risk women; R&R used typically with males with violent and sexual offences.

Debates: Social determinism (cognitions). Usefulness cannot be determined given methodological problems, programme content, incomplete delivery.

Link: Turning to Crime, Cognitions, e.g. Kohlberg and 'lack of moral development'; Freud an 'under-developed super-ego'.

Results: Comparison of 'before' and 'after' scores:
1. WBC: significant differences with experimental group, i.e. angry behaviours had decreased following course completion. Internal reliability of WBC was high (correlation co-efficients 0.97 for experimental and 0.93 for control group).
2. Prisoners' self-reports: indicated a significant decrease in anger following course completion (both measures at 1% significance).
3. Controls: no changes in scores on either measure.

Ireland, J. (2000) The impact of anger management programmes

Background: The need for anger management programmes arose because of disruptive/aggressive behaviour of prisoners. Developed in the UK in the late 1980s.

Aim: To assess the effectiveness of a brief group-based anger management programme.

Sample/participants: 87 male prisoners, mean age 18–19. 62% of experimental group and 68% of control/non-treatment group had been convicted for a violent offence.

Method/procedure: Quasi-(field) experiment (independent measures design). 50 in experimental group (received anger management), 37 controls (no treatment) group. Prisoners referred by prison officers/other staff /self. All pre-assessed. Prisoners completed an anger questionnaire (53 items, using rating scales, e.g. 'I have found it hard to control my anger', 0 = never, 2 = more than once) and their behaviour was assessed on the wing by prison officers using a wing-behaviour checklist (WBC) with a three-point scale: 0 = never shows behaviour, 2 = often shows behaviour (e.g. throws items about cell/wing; comes to office swearing/shouting) two weeks' prior to programme. Measures taken again eight weeks after the programme for both groups. The cognitive-behavioural programme comprised 12 one-hour group sessions run over a three-day period (group size *c.* 10, with two staff facilitators). Participants' tasks: keep anger diaries, contribute to group discussions, act in role-plays/group exercises, watch videos; complete homework. Sessions addressed anger triggers, consequences of anger and behaviour, thoughts/feelings; all videotaped; feedback provided to trained facilitators to ensure consistency in delivery.

Wheatley, M. (2007) Ear acupuncture's effectiveness in treating prisoners' drug addiction

Background: A high proportion of prison inmates have drug addictions/substance abuse problems on entry to prison.

Aim: To investigate the effectiveness of ear acupuncture in treating prisoners with a drug addiction.

Sample/participants: 350 prisoners in six high security UK prisons.

Method/procedure: Field experiment (independent measures design). Participants were screened to ensure there had been no substance abuse in 30 days prior to experiment and allocated to either an experimental group (who received ear acupuncture and basic standard care) or a control group (no treatment, just basic standard care). Experimental group received ear acupuncture (fine needles inserted in ear and they relaxed for *c.* 40 minutes) twice a week for four weeks; seen in groups (*c.* 10–15) by two trained practitioners. Prisoners completed questionnaires (covering background information; Alcohol Dependency Scale) and submitted to drug screening tests; staff recorded observations and completed reports on incidents.

Results: *Qualitative data:*

1. Self-reports of treated prisoners included sleeping better, improved psychological well-being, feeling better able to cope, reduced cravings (e.g. nicotine) and health improvements.
2. Observations by prison staff: noticed an overall calmer wing after treatment and noticed reduced demand for healthcare services (e.g. seeking medication to sleep).

Quantitative data:

1. 70% reduction in drug-related incidents (compared six months pre- to six months post-programme).
2. 41% reduction in serious, drug-related, incident reports (e.g. aggressive outbursts accompanied by physical violence against inmates/staff).
3. 42% reduction in positive mandatory drug testing results.
4. 33% reduction in positive voluntary drug testing results.

Evaluation: Large sample and more objective data (incident reports, etc.) and controls (e.g. drug testing) means study is more reliable. Although all high security prisoners, reasonable to assume these findings are generalisable across other categories of prisoners.

Debates: Social determinism/situational explanations of behaviour (effects of ear acupuncture). Useful technique beneficial beyond improvements relating to drug addiction (also relatively inexpensive) and does not depend on prisoners being highly motivated.

Extend

Research HM Prison Service for more information on treatment programmes. Go to: www.direct.gov.uk/en/index.htm and click on the 'Crime and justice' link.

Evaluation: Self-report measures, validity questionable (given likelihood of socially desirable responses; offenders have incentive to report improvement – consequences for parole, etc.) although WBC is an alternative data source and allows some check on validity (that is, if offenders self-report anger control improving, WBC scores should be in line/consistent). This triangulation also allows check on reliability. Sample size fairly reliable, although gender, age and crime-type restricted.

Debates: Social determinism/situational explanations of behaviour/nurture (anger management programme). Reductionist – does not investigate physiological factors (e.g. testosterone levels). Useful to maintain safer/less stressful environment (for both prisoners and staff).

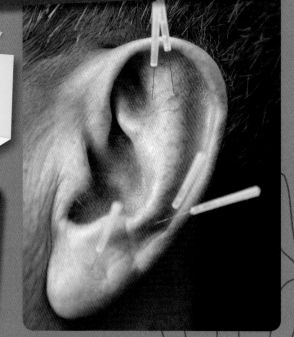

▲ **Figure 4.2** Ear acupuncture

HEALTH AND CLINICAL PSYCHOLOGY

5. Healthy living (see pp. 30–35)

Why do some people listen to healthy living messages while others do not? What is an effective health campaign? How can governments make people stick to their advice?

1. **Theories of health belief (HBM)**: behaviourist psychologists believe behaviour is maintained or changed by a process of positive and negative reinforcement. Rotter and Bandura both employ reinforcement as key parts of their theories of locus of control and self-efficacy. Lewin's Health Belief Model takes a cognitive approach, weighing up costs and benefits of taking a healthy action or not, but also acknowledges that social factors play a part.

2. **Methods of health promotion**: it is assumed that media campaigns work and huge amounts are spent on them by government but how effective are they? Is it better to just legislate for change when research suggests we should, as with cigarette advertising and car seat belts? Should we frighten people into obeying a health message or is this counter-productive? Drink-driving advertisements are very hard-hitting and seem to have produced a fall in this behaviour but how can change be maintained? Will people become immune to the fear message?

3. **Features of adherence to medical regimes**: examines what cognitive/behavioural psychology can be applied to explain why people do not stick to a healthy living message and actually change their lifestyles. How can we measure whether they do or not and in view of the massive NHS bill, how can psychologists help to improve adherence to medical advice?

6. Stress (see pp. 36–41)

How is stress measured? What causes it? What techniques work to reduce stress?

1. **Causes of stress**: many people are stressed because of their lifestyle and work and research has been done in the workplace to test how much effect this has. Life events and daily hassles have also been examined.

2. **Measuring stress**: looks at how psychologists have measured stress both physically and mentally and at how stress is affected by how much control a person feels they exert over whatever is stressing them.

3. **Techniques for managing stress**: cognitive and behavioural theories have been applied to the various techniques, with CBT now recognised as the treatment of choice for many anxiety and stress-related conditions. Bio-feedback is tested and the assumption that a good balance in life can reduce stress through increasing social contact is applied to aid survival from cancer.

7. Dysfunctional behaviour (see pp. 42–47)

How can psychologists define mental illness? How has this changed over time? What are the implications of diagnosing someone as mentally ill?

1. **Diagnosis of dysfunctional behaviour**: two main diagnostic manuals are used to diagnose a mental illness, the DSM-IV and the ICD-10. Both are undergoing revisions because of changing perceptions of what constitutes a disorder, which indicates the difficulties in putting a label on an invisible condition. Labelling is controversial and should at the very least be accurate, but research shows it can be affected by bias and culture.

2. **Explanations of dysfunctional behaviour**: classical conditioning is an early behaviourist explanation applied to the creation and treatment of phobias in Watson and Raynor's classic study. The hypothesis that mental illness has a genetic cause is tested in the twin study reported by Gottesman and Shields.

3. **Treatments for dysfunctional behaviour**: these often include pharmacotherapy. The efficacy of drugs alone are compared with combination therapies where cognitive therapy is applied to try to reverse negative thinking at the same time as the drugs hopefully enhance mood. Dysfunctional behaviour seems to be increasing so effective evidence-based therapies are essential to support patients and their families undergoing these conditions.

8. Disorders (see pp. 48–61)

What is the difference between the symptoms of the three main types of disorder? How are they explained and treated?

1. **Characteristics of disorders**: some specific disorders are described within the categories of anxiety, affective and psychotic disorders. In all cases, a behavioural, biological and cognitive explanation is described followed by three treatments from the same three approaches and perspectives.

2. **Explanations and treatments of an anxiety disorder: Phobias**: these are examined again to see if there is any biological predisposition to them or if they are all conditioned.

3. **Explanations and treatments of an affective disorder: Depression**: depression is a very common mental illness with great effects on the person concerned and their family. A behavioural, biological and combined approach to tackling the illness are examined.

4. **Explanations and treatments of a psychotic disorder: Schizophrenia**: the causes of schizophrenia have always been controversial and unclear. Behavioural evidence suggests some of the poor social skills of a schizophrenic could have been learnt. Twin studies are used to assess the biological evidence and the cognitive explanation of delusional thinking completes the conflicting research. Treatments for schizophrenia largely revolve around drugs but some evidence now suggests CBT can be very helpful.

THEORIES OF HEALTH BELIEF (HBM)

Becker, H. (1978) Compliance with a medical regimen for asthma: a test of the Health Belief Model

Aim: To use the Health Belief Model (HBM) to test mother's compliance to the medical regime for their children with asthma.

Background: Kurt Lewin's Health Belief Model has a phenomenological orientation, i.e. it is the patient who decides what he will or will not do and not the physical environment or the medical advice he or she receives. This depends on: 1) How likely the patient believes he or she will get a condition (perceived susceptibility); 2) The fear of the disease (perceived seriousness); 3) The patient's beliefs about the availability and effectiveness of treatment (perceived benefits); 4) A cue to action which could be internal (a change in a person's bodily state) or external (publicity about a disease); 5) Their age, sex, race, ethnicity, social class, peer groups and knowledge about the disease.

Sample: 111 mothers of children aged 9 months to 17 years.

Procedure: A correlational design was used with interview questions designed to provide measures of the HBM and how mothers had handled the latest asthma attack ('soft' measure). In addition, a covert blood test was taken to see if the asthma drug was in the child's system ('hard' measure).

Results: Eighty children's blood tests showed a 66.3% compliance rate. Becker and Rosenstock conclude that with both measures, mothers acted in ways predicted by the model. Mothers who feared that their child was vulnerable to a serious condition and that the asthma interfered with a child's activities were the more likely to comply. Reliability is high because it is consistently backed up by research which shows similar results each time. It supports a dispositional explanation of behaviour rather than a situational one because it is based on an individual's perception of their own state.

Debates: This behaviour seems more indicative of free will in action than a determinist viewpoint because the mothers seemed to be making choices about whether or not to medicate their children, although one could argue that it was the seriousness of the condition that had most effect. Usefulness – high because the model can be applied to many health problems; professionals who apply it will get greater compliance to medical advice.

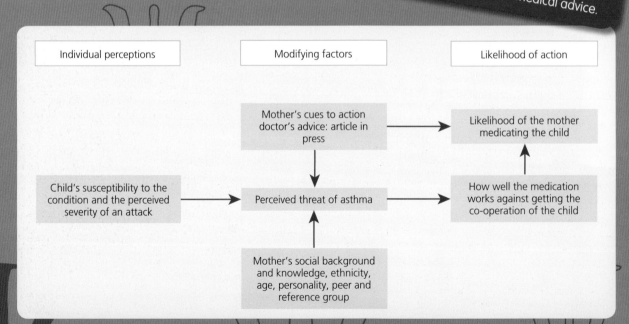

▲ **Figure 5.1** The Health Belief Model applied to a mother's likelihood of taking action to treat her child's asthma

Bandura, A. and Adams, N.E. (1977) Analysis of self-efficacy theory of behavioural change

Aim: To apply systematic desensitisation techniques to change a patient's self-efficacy so they come to believe they can cope with a threat.

Background: Bandura's theory of self-efficacy states that if a person believes that they can cope with a threat, they will use more effort and try for longer in the face of obstacles and unpleasant experiences. If they then master their fear, their self-efficacy further increases.

Sample/participants: 9 females and 1 male snake phobics aged19–57 with a mean age of 31 were recruited by advertisement.

Methods/procedure: A quasi-experiment. A series of pre-tests were given to the snake phobics to test their level of fear using rating scales of 1–10 for how frightened they would be to approach a boa constrictor in a case, to look down at it, touch it with gloves or bare hands, let it loose and catch it and hold it within 12 cm of their faces. Self-efficacy was tested by using a 100-point probability scale for how likely they felt they would succeed in the tasks above before they entered the room with the snake. 10 points on the scale was virtually impossible. They then received systematic desensitisation training including deep relaxation and visualisation of 51 scenes over about 4.5 hours.

Results: In the post test, the boa constrictor was used to test changes in self-efficacy and a corn snake used to see if self-efficacy generalised to other snakes. Bandura found that desensitisation reduced anxiety towards both threats and increased self-efficacy.

Evaluation: Laboratory experiment so high control and ability to test the effect of the IV (desensitisation) on the DV (fear and self-efficacy).

Debates: Supports an interactionist position in the nature/nurture debate. A person's self-efficacy is affected by personality and environment. It shows an interaction between free will and determinism. Usefulness – the theory can be widely applied to anxiety disorders.

Rotter, J.B. (1966) Generalized expectancies for internal versus external control of reinforcement

Aim: To test whether a reward is more effective if a person believes it came as a result of their own efforts (internal locus) or as a result of fate or chance (external locus).

Background: Rotter's theory suggests that if a person believes that reinforcement for behaviour is the result of their own efforts in either a positive or a negative way, it will strengthen their behaviour so they try harder or give up more quickly in a future similar situation. If he sees the behaviour as chance, it is less likely to be repeated. Applied to health, it could explain why some people repeatedly fail to lose weight by giving up on various diets when weight loss progress is slow. Similarly the fast results gained from using an inhaler for asthma is likely to lead to regular use and the belief that using medication works.

Sample/participants: 6 pieces of research in a review article.

Methods/procedure: Laboratory experiments using tasks such as line matching with very tiny differences, steady hand and extra sensory perception tasks. In one condition the participant thinks he is in control (skill-based); in the second condition there are both chance- and skill-based tasks. In both conditions participants are reinforced as right or wrong; however, success or failure is controlled by the experimenter.

Evaluation: There is much construct reliability as each of the six experiments supports the others and the original theory. Control is high with the laboratory experiment design so the IV and DV are clearly isolated and can determine a causal relationship. However, ecological validity is low with these artificial tasks. None of the six experiments have any health-related tasks or ill participants so generalising the results to health behaviour lacks mundane realism.

Debates: This is a determinist theory suggesting human behaviour can be manipulated by reinforcement. Supports nurture over nature. Shows an interaction between situational and dispositional factors.

Usefulness: When applied to health behaviour, it explains why some people carry on smoking when they know it will increase their risks of dying early. They may have an external locus of control and be trusting to luck.

Results: Behaviour changes are significantly greater when the participant believes their own skill causes their success or failure in a task. It also takes far longer for them to give up (extinguish behaviour).

METHODS OF HEALTH PROMOTION

Cowpe, C. (1989) Chip pan fire prevention 1976–1988

Aim: To demonstrate that advertising can make a valuable contribution to reducing the number of chip pan fire accidents.

Background: In the 1970s and early 1980s people commonly cooked chips at home in an open pan. These pans frequently caught fire. The two main causes were over filling, so they overflowed when the chips went in and unattendance, where the fat reached a flashpoint and ignited.

Sample/participants: TV viewers living in the Yorkshire Granada, Central, Tyne Tees and London regions where the adverts were shown were contacted.

Method: Field experiment.

Procedure: A TV campaign was produced with two 60-second commercials entitled 'Unattendance' and 'Overfilling'. Both showed the initial cause of the fire and then the actions needed to put it out: 1) Turn off the heat; 2) Cover with a damp cloth; 3) Leave the pan to cool down. To increase the dramatic effect, both slow motion and real-time filming was used.

Results: The overall results showed a net decline in fires of between 7% and 25% in twelve months with the greatest effect immediately after the campaign. Advertising awareness and recall also improved across the areas studied, suggesting that fires were being prevented by greater awareness of the risk and where a fire did occur it was contained and did not require the attendance of the fire brigade.

▲ Figure 5.2

Evaluation: This field experiment is high in ecological validity. People were at home so there were no demand characteristics. However, we do not know if the message was spread by the advertisements in every case because there is no control over who watched them.

Debates: This could be considered as a situational explanation rather than a dispositional one. Once people knew what to do, they could act accordingly.

Usefulness – the findings are useful because they show that if you want to change an unhealthy behaviour it is important to explain what to do rather than just what to avoid. Being informed gave people the power to act in a dangerous situation and saved lives.

Results: The overall response rate was 48.4%. Bicycle ownership was 85% on average across all three counties. Bicycle helmet use increased from 11.4% to 37.5% in Howard County after the law came in. This compared with 8.4% to 12.6% in Montgomery County, which used educational campaigns. Both were higher than the control group, Baltimore County.

Danneburg A.L. *et al.* (1993) Bicycle helmet laws and educational campaigns: An Evaluation of strategies to increase children's helmet use

Aim: To compare legislation against education to see which is more effective in increasing helmet use in child cyclists.

Background: The passage of a mandatory bicycle helmet law for children in Howard County, Maryland, USA provided an opportunity to compare legislation and education as strategies to increase helmet use. Head injuries cause death in 70% to 80% of all cycling accidents.

Sample: Children in the fourth, seventh and ninth grades in 47 schools in Maryland were tested across three counties. Over 2000 children at each age were asked to take part.

Method: This was a natural experiment with data collected by survey.

Procedure: Three counties were tested. Howard County, which brought in the legislation, Montgomery County, which used extensive educational campaigns and Baltimore County, which acted as the control with no particular measures to increase helmet use. Four- or five-point Likert scales were used in the survey questions, which were completed by the children without help from parents.

Results: The fear stimuli were effective with those in the high fear condition describing themselves as 'very worried'. There were no differences between the three groups in knowledge about tooth decay. One week later they were tested for conformity to the message and this time the moderate and minimal arousal groups had increased tooth brushing by 44% and 50% while the strong fear group had only changed by 28%.

Janis, I.L. and Feshbach, S. (1953) Effects of fear-arousing communications

Aim: To test the effects of fear arousal or anxiety by depicting potential dangers to which the audience might be exposed.

Background: Implicit in the use of fear appeals is the assumption that when emotional tension is aroused, the audience will become more highly motivated to listen. However, Janis and Feshbach believed that other types of defensive reactions to this fear might prevent the message from getting across.

Sample: 200 American high school students aged 14–16 divided into four groups at random. Three were experimental groups and one was the control.

Method: A laboratory experiment with an independent measures design.

Procedure: Three groups watched a 15-minute lecture delivered by the same speaker with the same content about the causes and prevention of tooth decay. Each lecture contained 20 slides which differed in the amount of fear they created. Immediately after the lecture, questionnaires were given out to test responses. The control group saw a lecture about the eye.

Evaluation: High levels of control gave the ability to manipulate the IV across four conditions. Measurement of the DV by questionnaire has possible problems of social desirability where respondents might wish to give what they perceive as the 'right' answer.

Debates: 'Is psychology a science?' could be used here because an apparently common sense idea has been repudiated through the use of the scientific method.

This research could be ethnocentric because Americans are renowned for caring about their teeth so the fear message could have had a stronger impact here than elsewhere. Usefulness – like Cowpe's research, this suggests that if you want to change behaviour you should inform people rather than frighten them.

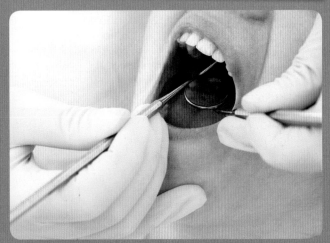

▲ **Figure 5.3** Janis and Feshbach's study tested the effects of fear when it came to tooth decay

Evaluation: Natural experiments have high external validity and low demand characteristics so we could expect that the findings were realistic. Young children may not understand the questions or may choose to give socially desirable answers, suggesting they did use their helmets when they did not. What about the majority who did not respond? Could they have been very different?

Debates: Free will vs. determinism – does society have the right to override our free choices? Situational vs. dispositional explanations – are some people natural risk takers whatever the situational variables? Usefulness – this research suggests that legislation may be more effective than educational campaigns and in some circumstances where lives are in danger it is justifiable to restrict personal freedom. An example is legislation on seat belts in the UK which dramatically reduced death and serious injury in car accidents.

FEATURES OF ADHERENCE TO MEDICAL REGIMES

Bulpitt, C. J. and Fletcher, A.E. (1988) The importance of wellbeing in hypertensive patients

Aim: To review research on the impact of being diagnosed with hypertension (high blood pressure), the effects of treatment and the factors influencing withdrawal from treatment.

Background: The main treatment for high blood pressure is to take diuretic drugs and to make lifestyle changes such as stopping smoking and drinking alcohol, reduce weight and reduce intake of salt and fat. This can make a patient feel a loss of wellbeing.

Sample: This review article reports on four surveys, a Medical Research Council (MRC) drug trial and various other studies. The data in the four surveys comes from 78 undiagnosed people who represent the baseline data against which to compare the responses of nearly 600 patients referred to doctors but not yet treated and over 800 treated patients.

Methods/procedure: Data was collected with self-administered questionnaires. In addition, some measures of urine sodium level excretion were taken to check if patients had in fact reduced their salt intake. The MRC drugs trial followed a randomised, single-blind format.

Results: The major reason people stopped treatment was the side effects; over the five years of the MRC trial, 15% withdrew with gout and impotence symptoms. Depression, lethargy and dizziness were also frequently reported. Labelling a patient as hypertensive had an effect on work and leisure by increasing absenteeism and increasing anxiety and patients were less likely to take part in hobbies due to tiredness and lethargy induced by the drug treatments.

Evaluation: A review article gives a wealth of data which covers several countries and gives a holistic picture of the effects of taking a medication for hypertension.
No two studies use the same methods so it is difficult to test reliability. Survey data could have problems with accuracy of memory and social desirability with patients exaggerating or minimising side effects of the drugs to be 'good' patients.
Debates: Psychology as a science: using results from randomised single blind drugs trials and incorporating with more qualitative data gives a rigorous picture. Usefulness – the findings should help medical practitioners be aware of the likely difficulties male patients in particular will have in taking these medications.

Lustman, P.J. *et al.* (2000) Fluoxetine for depression in diabetes: a randomised double-blind pacebo-controlled trial

Aim: To find out if treating depression in patients with diabetes with fluoxetine would work to help patients control their blood sugar levels and maintain their medication more effectively.

Background: Evidence suggests that the presence of diabetes doubles the risk of having depression and affects more than a quarter of people suffering from diabetes. Diabetic patients who are depressed are less likely to manage their condition well.

Sample/participants: 60 patients aged 21–65 years who met the diagnostic criteria for major depression. Each had a score of 14 or greater on the Beck Depression Inventory (BDI) or the Hamilton Rating Scale for Depression (HAMD). They had either Type 1 or Type 2 diabetes.

Methods: In the double-blind placebo-controlled study patients were randomly assigned to receive fluoxetine, which was initiated at a dosage of 20 mg per day and increased up to 40 mg daily as required by the clinical response. Depression and glycaemic control were evaluated during the third, fifth and eighth weeks of treatment.

Watt, P.M. *et al.* (2003) Funhaler spacer: Improving adherence without comprising on delivery

▲ **Figure 5.4** A funhaler

Aim: To see if inserting a fun device in an inhaler would improve adherence to the device by children.

Background: Poor adherence to taking their asthma medication is a problem for children with as few as 39% of children using their inhalers correctly and getting the right dose. This leads to more hospitalisations and greater risk of a very serious attack.

Sample/participants: 32 children (10 male, 22 female) aged 1.5–6 years with on average two years' suffering from asthma.

Methods/procedure: Data was collected by questionnaire two weeks after using the devices and they were completed by parents. The incentive toys (a whistle or spinner) were incorporated into the inhaler in a design which avoided any risk of contamination and which were intended to distract the child from the medication while at the same time encouraging the big breath needed to take in the drugs.

Results: An increase in use of 38% was reported, with more children likely to take the four cycles of delivery than with the standard device. The device was not affected by the insertion of the spacer and the same amount of medication was available in each 'puff'.

Evaluation: Collecting the data by questionnaire from parents could reveal a tendency to wish to report more use than actually happened, showing social desirability. Why only 38% improvement? This small sample of only 32 children is not very generalisable.

Debates: Difficulties with adherence to medical advice could be affected by culture so this research could be ethnocentric. Asthma is a western illness rarely found in the less developed world. Usefulness – a simple improvement which had a rapid effect at very little cost and showed a different approach was needed to get children to comply with medical advice.

Evaluation: A combination of psychometric test measures and blood tests makes the findings reliable. This was a small sample and results were taken after a relatively short time when it is well known that anti-depressants take some time to work. This is a rigorous design which restricts any bias.

Debates: This is a reductionist approach using alteration in brain chemistry through drugs to treat depression rather than looking at the whole lifestyle of the patient. Usefulness – provides evidence that adherence to a physical treatment could be affected by mental factors.

Results: Fifty-four of the 60 patients (27 in each group) completed the study. After eight weeks of fluoxetine therapy, depression scores had dropped significantly, from a mean BDI score of 23.6 to 9. In the placebo group, the mean BDI scores were 22.4 and 13.6 at baseline and after treatment, respectively. Improvement in HbA1c (blood glucose) level was greater in the fluoxetine group than in the placebo group, but the difference was not statistically significant. The mean decrease in HbA1c was 0.40% in the fluoxetine group and 0.07% in the placebo group. This shows a positive trend after eight weeks' treatment.

CAUSES OF STRESS

Johansson, G. *et al.* (1978) Social psychological and neuroendocrine stress reactions in highly mechanised work

Aim: To measure the amount of stress experienced by sawmill workers and to look for a causal relationship on work satisfaction and production.

Background: Modern production methods require constant attention to detail on monotonous repetitive production lines which have increased efficiency by requiring workers to specialise in particular tasks. However, this has led to low self-esteem and a lack of work satisfaction in the workforce, increasing stress-related illnesses.

Sample/participants: 14 high-risk workers, who cut, edged and graded the wood and a control group of 10 repair and maintenance workers. The mean age of both groups was 38.4. All were shift workers paid by piece rate based on group performance.

▲ Figure 6.1

Methods: This was a quasi-experiment where the workers fell naturally into the two groups.

Procedure: Work measures were collected four times a day through urine tests, body temperature and self-ratings of mood and alertness and consumption of caffeine and tobacco on the first or second day of the working week. These were compared to a day spent at home where workers were asked to stay up as if they were at work.

Results: Excretion of adrenaline in the urine of the high-risk workers was twice as high as the baseline and continued to increase to the end of the day, while the control group peaked in the morning then declined for the rest of the day. Self-reports showed the high-risk group feeling more rushed and irritated than the control group. More positive mood was reported by those doing the non-repetitive tasks.

Evaluation: Good reliability with the two methods supporting each other's findings. Good validity because it is a quasi-experiment in the field. Small sample and self-reports could mean problems with generalising these results to a wider sample in more interesting occupations.

Debates: Situational vs. individual explanations of behaviour – are some people more stress prone or is it situationally determined? Usefulness – useful to know how to improve conditions for factory workers. Moving them around the factory gives variety and therefore reduces monotony and stress.

Results: Top hassles were weight, health and money, while the main uplifts were good relationships with a partner and friends. Averaging over nine months of hassles, a correlation of 0.60 was found with psychological symptoms of stress, suggesting a strong relationship. There were differences between men and women with men showing a negative correlation (r = -0.18) between uplifts and a negative mood while women showed a positive correlation (r= 0.25). Hassles proved a stronger predictor of stress than life events.

Kanner, A.D. *et al.* (1981) Comparison of two modes of stress measurement: Daily hassles and uplifts versus major life events

Aim: To compare the Daily Hassles and Uplifts Scale versus the Major Life Events Scale to see if hassles were in fact the greater cause of stress.

Background: Kanner believed that it was not just the big events in life, but the many smaller daily events, such as bad traffic, queuing, being left on hold on a phone that add up to make us stressed. He believed that

Geer, J.H. and Maisel, E. (1972) Evaluating the effects of the prediction-control confound

Aim: Does lower stress result from being able to *predict* the occurrence of an unpleasant stimuli or is the lower stress related to the controlling behaviour itself?

Background: People prefer predictable rather than unpredictable averse events. By definition, people who control the termination of a stimulus can also predict its length. Therefore, people who can predict when an unpleasant event is going to stop should have a lower response to it.

Sample: 60 psychology undergraduates from New York University.

Method: A laboratory experiment involving three groups and using an independent measures design.

Procedure: The control group saw ten pictures of victims of violent death at 60-second intervals with a warning tone ten seconds before each one. They could press a button to change the picture as they wished. The 'predictability' and 'no control' group had no button and instead were 'yoked' to the control group. The 'predictability' group were unable to terminate or control the presentation but they knew about the relationship of the warning tone to the picture so they knew when it would come and how long it would last. The 'no control' group had no control and no idea how long each picture would last. They thought pictures and tones occurred at random. Data was collected by heart rate monitors and galvanic skin response via a polygraph.

Results: GSR results showed a clear difference between the prediction group and the other two, with a much greater stress response to the warning tone. There was no difference in response to the photographs between the predictability and no control groups but the control group itself showed a lower skin conductance. Therefore, being able to predict what was coming did not seem to prevent the stress response, whereas being able to stop it did. Heart rate monitors malfunctioned and were not included in the analysis.

Evaluation: These images may have caused distress to participants, breaching ethical guidelines. GSR is known to be unreliable as a polygraph test and the heart rate measures were also unreliable.

Debates: This was a poor reflection of 'psychology as a science' with weak generalisability and validity. It was low in usefulness and failed to clarify the mechanism involved in prediction and control of aversive stimuli.

a person can withstand a major event once in a lifetime far more easily than constant smaller ones. He also believed that uplifts such as feeling joy or good news had to be part of the picture.

Sample: 52 female and 48 men all White, who participated in a 12-month study of stress in Canada.

Methods/procedure: Each person took both the measures of stress above once a month for 9 months. They also completed the Hopkins Symptom Checklist (of stress symptoms) and the Bradburn Morale Scale of well-being towards the end of the study.

Evaluation: This was correlational data so shows relationships and not cause and effect. In the self-report data with scales, people may not be honest or may give socially desirable answers. There could be ethnocentric bias from the all-White sample.

Debates: Nature/nurture could be used here because stress is a built in 'flight or fight' response which could be more efficient in some people than others, or it could be an environmental response. Usefulness – using both hassles and uplifts give a more realistic picture of what actually happens to most people on a daily basis. Having a reliable scale is useful for doctors to quickly assess a patient's stress level and compare their score to a standardised score for a normal person.

MEASURING STRESS

Geer, J.H. and Maisel, E. (1972) Evaluating the effects of the prediction-control confound

This is the same study as the previous one on p. 37. You can use the research for both parts of the specification. In this part, you should focus on the measurements in particular. Two physical measures were used: the heart rate and the GSR. As described earlier, there were problems with the reliability of both measures.

Results: Very high agreement (>.90) was achieved between each group in the sample for each item. Males and females agreed, as did participants of various ages and religions. The lowest correlation was 0.82 between black and white individuals.

Evaluation: The usual issues with self-report techniques apply. However, the powerful agreement and large sample suggest this was a minor effect. Contrast with the hassles and uplifts scale: this has only the negative events and they are major and quite irregular.

Debates: Nature–nurture – are some people more prone to stress? Is it natural and do some people benefit? Items conformed to a western way of life so it could be seen as ethnocentric. Usefulness – the tool has been used by doctors for many years and can give a score of how much stress a person may have been subjected to in their recent past.

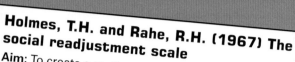

Holmes, T.H. and Rahe, R.H. (1967) The social readjustment scale

Aim: To create a method of measuring stress to take account of major events in a person's life.

Background: It is assumed that certain major life events such as marriage, bereavement and divorce are major stressors because they require change and cause disruption in a person's life. This has sometimes caused the onset of stress-related illnesses. A tool was needed which would give an idea of the scale of such disruption in people's lives so that doctors had some idea of the extent they were affecting their patients.

Sample: An opportunity sample of 394 people were used: 179 males and 215 females, of which 171 were single and 223 married. They were aged between 20 and 60 and were mainly middle class and White.

Method/procedure: A questionnaire containing 43 items was used. Each person assigned a value to various life events, starting with marriage which was given an arbitrary value of 500, and working down a list of 43 items. For each item, participants had to decide whether the event would need more or less readjustment than marriage. The final scores were then created by working out the mean values for the entire sample for each item. They were then put in order and the most stressful event – the death of a spouse was given a value of 100.

Johansson, G. et al. (1978) Social psychological and neuroendocrine stress reactions in highly mechanised work

This is the same study as used earlier on p. 36 and can be used for combined measures of stress because it used both physical and psychological measures. Work measures were collected through urine tests, body temperature and self-ratings of mood and alertness as well as consumption of caffeine and tobacco on the first or second day of the working week. These measures were compared to a day spent at home where the participants were asked to stay up as if they were at work. The same four times of day were used for the tests in both conditions.

TECHNIQUES FOR MANAGING STRESS

▲ **Figure 6.2** Exams can be stressful

Meichenbaum, D.H. (1972) Cognitive modification of test anxious college students

Aim: To compare a group of anxious students receiving cognitive modification with a group being treated by desensitisation and a control group waiting for therapy.

Background: Anxious people are known to ruminate over their performance, feel inadequate and anticipate negative outcomes when exposed to a test. This worrying is thought to be more of a problem for patients than the emotional response. Stress Inoculation Therapy (SIT) directly tackles the negative thinking and replaces it with positive thinking and relaxation strategies.

Sample/participants: 21 volunteers who responded to an advert in a university newspaper for 'treatment of test anxiety' participated. Most were undergraduates.

Method: Laboratory experiment using a matched pairs design and three groups.

Procedure: Participants were pretested for anxiety levels by a laboratory-based anxiety adjective test, an IQ test and test anxiety questionnaire and then assigned to one of the groups so that each group had equally anxious students. They all received eight sessions of treatment except the control group. The SIT group had insight training and the systematic desensitisation group had progressive relaxation and imagery techniques. Grade averages, IQ and digital performance tests and self-reports post treatment were the measurement of the DV. The experimenters were blind to the conditions participants had been assigned to.

Results: The two therapy groups both improved but were not significantly different from each other on the grade averages, digital symbols and the IQ test. On the self-report of test anxiety, the SIT group showed the most positive change. It was concluded that cognitive therapy was most helpful in test anxious students.

Evaluation: Could a sample of university undergraduates be more responsive to a cognitive solution because they will be more able to express their worries and more likely to practise the skills needed because they are highly motivated to pass tests?

Debates: Ethnocentrism – is this research a feature of westernised society? Usefulness – cognitive therapy has been shown to be effective in many other anxiety disorders but does require the patient to be convinced it will work.

Budzynski, T. et al. (1973), EMG biofeedback and tension headache: A controlled outcome study

Aim: To test the effectiveness of bio-feedback techniques in reducing headaches.

▲ **Figure 6.3** Undergoing bio-feedback

Background: Tension headaches are associated with sustained contraction of the scalp and neck muscles. In this case auditory tones are used to feedback to patients as they relax their tight muscles: the lower the tone, the greater the relaxation.

Sample/participants: 18 patients volunteered to take part after responding to an advert. They were screened for having tension headaches only, with no other problems.

Method: A laboratory experiment was used with an independent measures design. Group A had biofeedback sessions which included relaxation training and EMG feedback (information on muscle tension). Group B had relaxation training with pseudo-feedback (a tape recording from someone else's session with no link to them personally – a control for 'noise'). Group C were told they were on a waiting list but had to come to appointments to remain in the study (a control for attention).

Procedure: For two weeks, patients kept a diary of their headaches, rating them on a scale of 1 (mild) –5 (severe) to provide baseline data. They also completed the MMPI which tested depression, hysteria and hypochondria. Group A had 16 sessions of training twice a week for eight weeks. They were told that slower clicks of the machine indicated less muscle tension and had to practise at home twice a day for 15–20 minutes. Group B were just told to listen to the clicks. All patients kept a record of their headaches while on the program.

Results: Group A's muscle tension was significantly lower than Group B's and their headaches were significantly less too. The MMPI showed lower levels of hysteria and depression at the end of the study for all the groups but only the experimental group showed less hypochondriasis. Drug usage fell and the effects persisted even 18 months later.

Evaluation: Ethically sound because both control groups were offered treatment in the end. High control and use of psychometric data with the muscle relaxation and diary entries providing good reliability. Validity also improved as the technique is used at home.

Debates: Free will vs. determinism – how much is illness under our own free will? Do people choose to be ill or choose to be well? Is illness always determined by external factors? Usefulness – biofeedback appears to be an effective technique and useful for teaching relaxation. It is relatively cheap and has no side effects so can be widely prescribed for stress-related conditions.

Waxler- Morrison, N. *et al.* (1991) Effects of social relationships on survival for women with breast cancer: a prospective study

Aim: To look at predictors of survival from cancer including social support from friends and family.

Background: It appears that women who tend to survive longest from cancer are those who are hostile to the diagnosis and uncooperative with their doctors, while those who stoically accept the diagnosis tend to die earlier. This indicates that there is a big psychological component to the illness.

Sample: 133 women who were referred with breast cancer under the age of 55 to a clinic in Vancouver. They were similar in their pathology.

Method: A quasi-experiment where the women fell naturally into their categories.

Procedure: The women completed a questionnaire to obtain demographic and psychosocial data such as how many dependants they had, how many friends, etc. Clinical factors were taken from the patients' medical records by a clerk. Survival was calculated from time of diagnosis. Finally, 18 patients were interviewed in detail to fully understand the effects of the psychosocial factors.

Results: Six of eleven aspects of social network were significantly associated with survival. They were: marital status, support from friends, contact with friends, total support, employment status and social network. From the interviews it appeared that practical help was the most useful, such as cooking, childcare and shopping. Complex relationships with young adult children were the least supportive with women feeling that they had to support them by remaining cheerful. Marital status was very important, particularly with the husband's reaction to mastectomy. Earlier research about involvement in social activities, degree of extraversion and anger were not significant in this study against the six key findings.

Evaluation: The method is strong with a large sample and data was gathered directly from the patients. However, restricting the sample to those aged below 55 rules out the most 'at risk' group of older women who may have very different social lives.

Debates: Situational vs. dispositional explanations of behaviour – it seems one's disposition or personality is less important than external or situational factors in helping to survive cancer, despite earlier findings. Usefulness – very useful research which shows how support group could be key to survival and also that the whole family is part of the healing process.

◀ **Figure 6.4** Marital status was found to be very important in cancer survival rates

DIAGNOSIS OF DYSFUNCTIONAL BEHAVIOUR

The Diagnostic Statistics Manual DSM and the International Classification of Disorders (ICD) (Allpsych Online – www.allpsych.com)

Aim: To find a way of categorising mental illness that could be applied by any psychiatrist.

Background: Two main classification systems are used to diagnose mental illness in most of the world. Both systems are now under revision and both are very controversial. As yet there are no biological tests for mental illness although some are in development. A simple comparison of the two systems is shown in Table 7.1 below.

▼ **Table 7.1** Summary comparison of the two diagnostic criteria used in the western world

DSM-IV - American	ICD-10 - World Health Organisation
Axis 1: Clinical disorders, e.g. alcohol abuse	Each disorder is listed in one of 11 categories
Axis 2: Personality disorders, e.g. histrionic	Personality disorders are category 9
Axis 3: General medical conditions, e.g. cancer or diabetes effects on mood	Medical conditions are covered in the first category
Axis 4: Psychosocial and environmental problems, e.g. stressful events like divorce	Built into the groupings of the disorders are the causal factors such as organic cause, substance abuse and stress
Axis 5: Global assessment of functioning, e.g. How well is the patient working?	There is no global assessment of functioning separately

Supporting research: See the Ford and Widiger study opposite for research which has used the DSM-III system to categorise mental illness. You could also use Rosenhan's study 'On being sane in insane places' from AS Psychology.

Evaluation: Psychiatrists do not always agree on a diagnosis using the same systems. This is because symptoms overlap and occur in clusters with no clear boundaries. Diagnosis depends on the clinical interview and this in turn depends on how honest and open the patient is about their symptoms. A high proportion of mental illnesses are diagnosed 'unspecified' in ICD-10 or 'not otherwise specified' in DSM-IV. This suggests the criteria are not working well. Cultural changes affect inclusion of symptoms, e.g. homosexuality has been removed.

Debates: Nature vs. nurture – are mental illnesses inherited or learnt? Free will vs. determinism – at what point does a mentally ill person lose free will? Psychology as a science – where is the science in diagnosis? Why no hard and fast tests? Usefulness – the new systems will be more descriptive and will increase validity because a long process of discussion is going on world-wide to agree the new categories.

Rosenhan, D.I. and Seligman, M.E.P. (1995) Defining Abnormality

Aim: To try to define what we mean by someone who is abnormal generally.

Background: Rosenhan has attempted to define what we mean by abnormality:

Statistical infrequency: for instance one may say that an individual who has an IQ below or above the average level of IQ in society is abnormal.

Violation of social norms: a person's thinking or behaviour is classified as abnormal if it violates the (unwritten) rules about what is expected or acceptable behaviour in a particular social group.

Failure to function adequately: an individual may be unable to perform the behaviours necessary for day-to-day living, e.g. self-care, hold down a job.

Rosenhan and Seligman (1989) suggest the following characteristics that define failure to function adequately: suffering; maladaptiveness (danger to self); vividness and unconventionality (stands out); unpredictability and loss of control; irrationality/incomprehensibility; causes observer discomfort; violates moral/social standards.

Deviation from ideal mental health: under this definition, we define what is normal (Macleod 2008) and anything that deviates from this is regarded as abnormal. Normality is a: positive view of the self; capability for growth and development; autonomy and independence; accurate perception of reality; positive friendships and relationships; environmental mastery – able to meet the varying demands of day-to-day situations.

Ford, M.R. and Widiger, T.A. (1989) Sex bias in the diagnosis of histrionic and antisocial personality disorders

Aim: To assess whether sex bias is prevalent in diagnosis of mental disorders and if this can be minimised by the explicit criteria in the DSM-III manual.

Background: There is a difference in the number of males and females diagnosed with histrionic personality disorder (HPD) and antisocial personality disorders (APD). This has been attributed to sex bias.

Sample: 354 psychologists. Of these, 76% were men with an average of 15.6 years of experience using a variety of therapies.

Method: This was a self-report where psychologists responded to a series of case histories and made a diagnosis using DSM-III criteria.

Procedure: The 266 psychologists were given one of nine case histories involving a female, a male or a sex-unspecified patient each time. The case histories included the symptoms needed by the DSM-III for the unique diagnosis of APD or HPD or they were mixed together in the 'balanced' histories. The psychologists used 7-point scales to say how confident they were the patient had each condition. An independent panel of 88 psychologists rated how closely the case histories were examples of a histrionic or antisocial condition.

Results: The sex-unspecified group was mostly diagnosed with borderline personality disorder and not particularly APD or HPD. The individual lists of symptoms were found to be 80% representative of APD and HPD by the panel of 88 and there were no male/female differences found in the lists. With HPD, males were 44% and females 76% more likely to be diagnosed with the condition. With APD, females were 15% and males 42% more likely to be diagnosed with the condition. Male and female psychologists were equally likely to make these diagnoses. This showed clearly the bias in diagnosis when all else was controlled.

Evaluation: The unbalanced sample of only 24% females could be a problem for calculating male/female differences in the clinicians themselves.

Debates: Psychology as a science – difficulty of agreed diagnosis by psychologists from a variety of backgrounds suggests the process is not very scientific. Ethnocentrism – clearly cultural beliefs about the roles of men and women affected diagnosis in this study. Usefulness – the fact that the individual behaviour lists did not elicit a sex bias suggests that it is the label of the illness itself which causes a stereotyped response and this is important in future labelling of illnesses in the revisions of these manuals.

Evaluation: Many very gifted individuals could be classified as 'abnormal' using this definition. Some characteristics are regarded as abnormal even though they are quite frequent, e.g. depression may affect one in five of the elderly (MHF, 2001). This would make it common but that does not mean it is not a problem. Drink driving was once considered acceptable but is now seen as socially unacceptable whereas homosexuality has gone the opposite way. Many people engage in behaviour that is maladaptive/harmful or threatening to self, but we do not class them as abnormal, e.g. adrenaline sports.

Debates: Is psychology a science? Why are there no agreed biological or clinical tests for abnormality yet? No definitive agreement between practitioners weakens the credibility of the subject. Ethnocentrism – is abnormality as we know it a westernised idea? Are mentally ill people seen differently in other parts of the world? Usefulness – there are problems with every definition and some people argue that we are all on a continuum for most behaviour.

EXPLANATIONS OF DYSFUNCTIONAL BEHAVIOUR

Gottesman, I.J. and Shields, J.A. (1976) A critical review of recent adoption, twin and family studies of schizophrenia: behavioural genetics perspectives

Aim: To review research on family, twin and adoption studies to test for evidence of a genetic cause.

Background: A dispute had arisen between those who believed that schizophrenia was caused by environmental factors such as schizophrenic or abnormal parenting and those who believed there was a genetic cause. Twin and adoption studies begun in the late 1960s attempted to resolve the issue.

Sample: In total there were 711 participants in the adoption studies and 210 monozygotic twins and 317 dizygotic twin sets studied.

Method: A review article of three adoption and five twin studies between 1967 and 1976.

Procedure: Concordance rates (how often both twins were diagnosed with schizophrenia) and incidence of schizophrenia in parents and children in biological and adoptive families were calculated in the studies.

Results: All three adoption studies showed increased incidence of schizophrenia in adopted children with a schizophrenic biological parent, but normal children fostered with a schizophrenic parent did not develop schizophrenia. In one study, the biological siblings of children with schizophrenia were found to have a 19.2% chance of also developing the condition. The twin studies also supported the biological explanation, with monozygotic twins showing a 58% concordance rate compared to 12% in dizygotic twins.

Evaluation: Both genes and environment are each necessary but not sufficient for developing schizophrenia. There were disagreements on the diagnosis of schizophrenia across the studies. No single gene for schizophrenia has been identified.

Debates: Nature/nurture is a clear debate here with the use of twin studies which offer the possibility to test genes against environment. Once again, reliability of diagnosis could be an issue here. Usefulness – the research suggests potential genetic cures but a need to isolate many genes first and also to investigate environmental causes, as yet unspecified, although cannabis is one suspect at the moment.

Results: Within the first week, Albert showed fear towards the rat and this got worse over seven sessions so that just the rat with no noise produced a strong response. The fear then transferred to a rabbit, a dog, a seal-fur coat, some cotton wool, Watson's hair and a Santa Claus mask to varying degrees. Building blocks were used as a neutral stimulus and they had the effect of calming Albert between the stressful presentations. He was removed from the hospital before they could test whether they could remove the fear.

Watson, J.B. and Rayner, R. (1920) Conditioned emotional reactions

Aim: To see if a conditioned fear response could be created in a previously normal child by using classical conditioning. Would the fear transfer to other objects and what would happen over time? Could the fear later be removed?

Background: Watson and Rayner wanted to find out how simple emotional responses in childhood such as fear, rage and love became the more complete adult rage of behaviours and believed that classical conditioning had a role to play.

Sample: A nine-month-old child, Albert, who was the son of a wet-nurse employed at the hospital where Watson worked. He was described as 'stolid' which means calm and unemotional.

Method: A controlled experiment conducted as a case study.

Procedure: First a fear response was discovered in Albert which was the sound of a metal bar being struck close to the child. Then this feared sound was paired with the presentation of a white rat which the child had previously played happily with. This process was repeated over approximately six weeks with variations.

Beck, A.T. (1961) A systematic investigation into depression

Aim: To understand how people with depression think and how their thinking differs from normal people.

Background: People with depression often have low self-esteem, criticise themselves a lot and blame themselves for failures which other people see as illogical and without any basis in fact. This leads to a gradual withdrawal from other people and a failure to enjoy things once enjoyed. At its worst, suicidal thoughts of escape from a pointless life predominate.

Sample: 50 patients diagnosed with depression – 16 men and 34 women with a median age of 34. Twelve were diagnosed as having psychotic-depressive or manic-depressive reactions and 38 as having neurotic-depressive reactions.

Method: Clinical interviews in a matched pairs design as the patients were compared to a control group of non-depressed people matched for age, sex and social position.

Procedure: Clinical interviews using free association, formal analysis and diaries of thoughts were used to collect the data and patients were asked about their thoughts before the interview and during the interview. The non-depressed patients also recorded their thoughts for comparison.

Results: There were clear differences between the two groups in certain themes of low self-esteem, self-blame, overwhelming responsibilities and a desire to escape. They felt anxiety by feeling they were in personal danger, a hypomanic state by themes of self-enhancement and a hostile paranoid state by themes of accusations against others. In addition there was a tendency to ruminate at length on failures. In all cases there was no logical basis for these feelings.

Evaluation: Collecting data in a therapeutic relationship lacks reliability and increases the likelihood of bias. The use of free association could have 'fed' negative ideas to the patients.

Debates: Freewill vs. determinism – do patients consciously choose to think like this or is their condition determined by external factors in their lives? Reductionism – reduces depression to illogical thinking. Usefulness – because it supports other similar research the findings are useful, but it lacks rigour and reliability. It provides an alternative to biological explanations which rely on drug-based therapies.

Evaluation: Watson justified the stress on the child by saying sooner or later this sort of thing would happen to him in real life. The study showed how powerful classical conditioning can be in explaining phobias.

Debates: Nature/nurture debate could be used here. Watson's work is clearly on the nurture side of this debate. Contrast with the evolutionary perspective of 'preparedness'. Situational vs. dispositional explanations of behaviour could also be discussed. Was Albert's behaviour the result of his situation or his personality? Usefulness – provides an explanation and through systematic desensitisation, a cure for phobias.

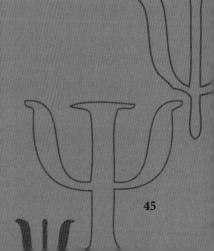

TREATMENTS FOR DYSFUNCTIONAL BEHAVIOUR

Karp, J.F. and Frank, E. (1995) Combination therapy and the depressed woman

Aim: To compare drug treatment or therapy alone, with a combination of drugs and therapy for depression in women.

Background: Following the early enthusiasm for anti-depressants, many clinicians realised they did not alleviate all the symptoms of depression. One hypothesis is that adding therapy to a drug regimen will build a relationship which in turn would improve adherence to medication. Similarly, including the patient's family helps patients to stay on the drugs long enough for them to work.

Sample: Various samples of women and men with depression from 1974 to 1992 who met the DSM criteria for a major depressive episode.

Method: A review of many studies which had mainly two conditions, either drug and placebo or therapy and placebo or therapy plus drugs. Some would have been matched pairs designs.

Procedure: Depression was analysed using inventories such as the Beck Depression Inventory (BDI) and patients were tested before and after treatment. Each study followed differing procedures depending on their focus, e.g. one study looked at life events using the Bedford College Life Events and Difficulties Schedule (LEDS).

Results: Very little evidence was found to support the effectiveness of combination therapy over either therapy or drug therapy alone for women patients. Some evidence would seem to support the idea that seeing a therapist regularly helps both men and women stick to their medication. Women planning pregnancies should use therapy alone as this was as effective as drugs.

Evaluation: A huge amount of data is evaluated but all from differing methodologies and scales so it is hard to determine reliability. People become depressed for many different reasons and so the routes to recovery are likely to be equally as varied.

Debates: Individual vs. situational explanations of behaviour – are some people more likely to have depression because of their personalities or is it caused by environmental influences. Ethnocentrism – is this a disease of developed countries? Is our tendency to label it as an illness correct? Usefulness – not particularly useful because it is not conclusive, although failure to find differences between men and women might reduce stereotyping of women as neurotic.

Results: Balloon bursting was the first fear to be tackled and by the fourth session, Lucy could bear it being popped 10 metres away quite calmly. In the fifth session she was able to pop the balloon herself. The other feared objects were then introduced and by the tenth session her fear thermometer scores had dropped from 7/10 to 3/10 for balloons popping and fear of the cap gun from 8/10 to 5/10.

McGrath, T. *et al.* (1990) Successful treatment of a noise phobia in a nine-year-old girl with systematic desensitisation *in vivo*

Aim: To treat a girl with a noise phobia using systematic desensitisation.

Background: Fear of loud noises is common in children but for some it impacts on normal life. Lucy, the girl in this study, could not go to parties and school trips or anywhere where fireworks might go off.

Sample: Lucy was a nine-year-old of low average intelligence (IQ 97). She showed as averagely depressed, fearful and anxious when she was tested and therefore it was felt her fear of noise was not part of a wider condition and could be treated.

Method: Systematic desensitisation was used and written up as a case study.

Procedure: Lucy was taught to relax and then she created a hierarchy of feared noises including doors banging, cap-guns popping, balloons bursting and unexpected explosions of party poppers. Imagining herself at home with her toys, on her bed and deep breathing was used to control her fear. She also used a fear thermometer, rating her fear from 1 to 10. As she was given the feared object, she paired it with the relaxation and imagery she had learnt until she was calm.

Lam, D.H. *et al.* (2003) A randomised controlled study of cognitive therapy for relapse prevention for bipolar affective disorder

Aim: To test whether patients with bipolar affective disorder could be helped with cognitive therapy (CT) to prevent relapses.

Background: Beck's cognitive therapy (CT) seeks to help the patient overcome difficulties by identifying and changing dysfunctional thinking, behaviour and emotional responses. Therapy may consist of testing the assumptions which one makes and identifying how certain of one's usually unquestioned thoughts are distorted, unrealistic and unhelpful. Beck initially focused on depression and developed a list of 'errors' in thinking that he proposed could maintain depression, including exaggerating negatives and minimising of positives.

Sample: 103 patients with Bipolar 1 disorder according to DSM-IV, who experienced frequent relapses despite using mood stabilisers, were invited to take part. They were averagely affected by their illness with no extreme sufferers in the sample.

Method: A single-blind randomised controlled study with an independent measures design.

Procedure: Patients were randomised into a CT group or control group by computer program. Both the control and CT groups received mood stabilisers and regular psychiatric follow-up. In addition, the CT group received an average of 14 sessions of CT during the first six months and two booster sessions in the second six months. Independent assessors, blind to the conditions, assessed the patients at six-month intervals against DSM-IV criteria for a relapse, and monthly for depression scores, and questionnaires about levels of social functioning.

Results: During the 12-month period, the CT group had significantly fewer bipolar episodes, days in a bipolar episode, and number of admissions for this type of episode. The CT group also had significantly higher social functioning. During these 12 months, the CT group showed fewer mood symptoms on the monthly mood questionnaires. Furthermore, there was significantly less fluctuation in manic symptoms in the CT group. The CT group also coped better with manic prodromes (early warning of an episode) at 12 months.

Evaluation: There was no control for the amount of attention received by the CT group or medication prescribed, or any control over sleep routines. This was a well-constructed study, free from experimenter bias in its analysis.

Debates: Freewill and determinism – this study raises the question that if a patient can use cognitive control to improve symptoms, does that mean that mental illnesses are always under our control? This study shows that psychology can be scientific in the way research is conducted. Usefulness – the study shows a clear benefit for using CT with pharmacotherapy with moderately affected patients suffering from bipolar disorder.

Evaluation: Systematic desensitisation seems to be highly replicable with many different patients and conditions. Giving the patient control over timing increased the effectiveness, which is interesting because it introduces a cognitive component to a behavioural theory.

Debates: Freewill vs. determinism could be used because this study suggests our conscious control can be used to treat fears and phobias. Reductionism could be explored because it reduces a phobia to a learned response. Psychology as a science – this could be a demonstration of a scientific approach to a treatment. Usefulness – a very useful treatment with many applications.

Affective – bipolar

Edited DSM-IV criteria for a major depressive episode:

Five (or more) of the following symptoms have been present during the same two-week period and represent a change from previous functioning:

- Depressed mood most of the day, nearly every day, as indicated by either subjective report (e.g. feels sad or empty) or observation made by others (e.g. appears tearful).
- Markedly diminished interest or pleasure in all, or almost all, activities most of the day, nearly every day (as indicated by either subjective account or observation made by others).
- Significant weight loss when not dieting or weight gain (e.g. a change of more than 5% of body weight in a month), or decrease or increase in appetite nearly every day.
- Insomnia or hypersomnia nearly every day.
- Psychomotor agitation or retardation nearly every day (observable by others, not merely subjective feelings of restlessness or being slowed down).
- Fatigue or loss of energy nearly every day.
- Feelings of worthlessness or excessive or inappropriate guilt (which may be delusional) nearly every day (not merely self-reproach or guilt about being sick).
- Diminished ability to think or concentrate, or indecisiveness, nearly every day (either by subjective account or as observed by others).
- Recurrent thoughts of death (not just fear of dying), recurrent suicidal ideation without a specific plan, or a suicide attempt or a specific plan for committing suicide.

In addition, the symptoms cause clinically significant distress or impairment in social, occupational or other important areas of functioning and are not due to taking drugs or a physical illness or a recent bereavement. The symptoms must persist for longer than two months or are characterised by marked functional impairment, morbid preoccupation with worthlessness, suicidal ideation, psychotic symptoms or psychomotor retardation.

Anxiety – phobia

Edited DSM-IV criteria for phobias:

- Marked and persistent fear that is excessive or unreasonable, cued by the presence or anticipation of a specific object or situation (e.g. flying, heights, animals, receiving an injection, seeing blood).
- Exposure to the phobic stimulus almost invariably provokes an immediate anxiety response, which may take the form of a panic attack.
- The person recognises that the fear is excessive or unreasonable.
- The phobic situation(s) is avoided or else is endured with intense anxiety or distress. The avoidance, anxious anticipation or distress in the feared situation(s) interferes significantly with the person's normal routine, occupational (or academic) functioning, or social activities or relationships, or there is marked distress about having the phobia.
- In individuals under age 18 years, the duration is at least six months.
- The anxiety, panic attacks or phobic avoidance associated with the specific object or situation are not better accounted for by another mental disorder, such as obsessive–compulsive disorder (e.g. fear of dirt in someone with an obsession about contamination), post-traumatic stress disorder (e.g. avoidance of stimuli associated with a severe stressor), separation anxiety disorder (e.g. avoidance of school), social phobia (e.g. avoidance of social situations because of fear of embarrassment), panic disorder with agoraphobia or agoraphobia without history of panic disorder.

You need to be familiar with all of the disorders described. Evaluation follows all three disorders.

Evaluation of the characteristics of disorders:

The DSM criteria are criticised for lacking validity and being vague. It is possible for a misdiagnosis to occur because people do not need to show all the symptoms for a disorder and for only short periods of time. Symptoms overlap, e.g. the negative symptoms of schizophrenia are very similar to those of depression. Similarly, mania in bipolar disorder could be confused with positive symptoms of schizophrenia. The use of the criteria is affected by what a therapist might consider a 'normal' life, which is bound to be affected by cultural norms and stereotypes about what men and women are like. The therapist has only observation, the patient's word or the views of relatives to go on in the clinic and a patient may appear very different in a clinical setting to how they appear at home. Some people have argued that mental illness is a myth and disorders are just general variations of people along a continuum (Szasz 1960). Rosenhan and Seligman's (1973) research also showed difficulties in diagnosis and the unreliability of clinical practice. Labelling someone as a depressive or phobic has negative associations.

Debates: Ethnocentrism – is mental illness culturally determined? Are the values we place on a healthy life biased towards a western perspective? Nature /nurture – does some mental illness run in families? Or is the Diasthesis–Stress model more accurate by explaining behaviour as a result of both biological and genetic vulnerability and stress from life experiences? Usefulness – diagnosing disorders can give people a relief from wondering why they do not enjoy life and can give them the treatment they need to help them over their problems. Having a diagnosis can have legal uses too.

Psychotic – schizophrenia

Edited DSM-IV criteria for schizophrenia:

Criterion A: Characteristic symptoms

Two (or more) of the following, each present for a significant portion of time during a one-month period (or less if successfully treated):

- delusions
- hallucinations
- disorganised speech
- grossly disorganised or catatonic behaviour
- negative symptoms, i.e., affective flattening, alogia or avolition

(NB. Only one Criterion A symptom is required if delusions are bizarre or hallucinations consist of a voice keeping up a running commentary on the person's behaviour or thoughts, or two or more voices conversing with each other.)

Criterion B: Social/occupational dysfunction

For a significant portion of the time since the onset of the disturbance, one or more major areas of functioning such as work, interpersonal relations, or self-care are markedly below the level achieved prior to the onset (or when the onset is in childhood or adolescence, failure to achieve expected level of interpersonal, academic or occupational achievement).

Criterion C: Duration

Continuous signs of the disturbance persist for at least six months. This six-month period must include at least one month of symptoms (or less if successfully treated) that meet Criterion A (i.e. active-phase symptoms) and may include periods of prodromal or residual symptoms. During these prodromal or residual periods, the signs of the disturbance may be manifested by only negative symptoms or two or more symptoms listed in Criterion A present in an attenuated form (e.g. odd beliefs, unusual perceptual experiences).

Criterion D: No other explanation

No other disorder is identified at the same time, no drug abuse or medication could explain the behaviour and there was no other developmental disorder.

EXPLANATIONS AND TREATMENTS OF AN ANXIETY DISORDER: PHOBIAS

You are required to choose only ONE disorder (either affective or anxiety or psychotic) and follow it through its explanations and treatments (there is no need to do more). Explanations of an anxiety disorder are given below.

Phobia explanations – Behavioural

See Watson and Raynor on page 44 for this explanation which uses Classical Conditioning.

Phobia explanations – Biological

Ahman, A. *et al*., (1975) Phobias and preparedness: phobic versus neutral pictures as conditioned stimuli for human autonomic responses

Aim: Using classical conditioning to investigate whether a phobia of snakes could be conditioned more easily than a neutral stimulus such as a house or face.

Background: Evolutionary psychology would predict that we should be more biologically predisposed to fear snakes from an ancient survival instinct than electric sockets or cars, which are actually more likely to kill us in the present day. Evolutionary theory put survival at the heart of human behaviour and even today we are affected by this biological instinct.

Sample: 64 paid volunteers: 38 females and 26 males, all psychology students and with an average age of 25.

Method/procedure: Laboratory experiment with an independent measures design with three conditions. Participants had electrodes attached to the first and second fingers of their right hand, which could deliver an electric shock described as uncomfortable but not painful. On their left hand they had skin conductance electrodes on the first and second finger. The participants watched slides of snakes, houses and faces. The phobic group were shocked every time they saw a snake and the neutral groups were shocked when they saw houses or faces. The control group saw snakes but were not shocked. In the extinction phase of the experiment, the electrodes were disconnected and the experimenter informed the participants there would be no more shocks

Results: At the start of the experiment all the groups had the same skin conductance rate of around 0.017 (log micromhos), but the phobic group went up to 0.062 compared with the houses and faces group, who went up to 0.048. The control group who were not shocked went up to 0.037. The phobic group also showed more resistance to extinction.

Evaluation: There is a strong expectancy effect here with the control group showing a strong response with no shock being given. If you take that away from the response of the experimental group, the results are less impressive. The method is reliable but probably lacks a lot of ecological validity because it is so artificial.

Debates: Nature/nurture debate. Contrast this study with Watson and Raynor's study of Little Albert. Usefulness – the study offers the possibility of providing an experimental means of testing different methods of treatment.

Phobia explanations – Cognitive DiNardo, P.A. (1998) Generalised Anxiety Disorder

Aim: To see if excessive worry was a reliable symptom of Generalised Anxiety Disorder (GAD) and could be included in the revision of the DSM-III to version IV.

Background: When the diagnostic systems are revised, a lot of debate takes place over the experimental evidence available to include particular symptoms which will reliably distinguish one disorder from another. Di Nardo wanted to find additional reliability for the inclusion of excessive worry in GAD.

Sample: The total sample was 145 patients, of whom 53 had GAD.

Method/procedure: This was a quasi-experiment on patients attending one of three clinics in Eastern USA. Two independent interviews were administered to each patient using the Anxiety Disorders Interview Schedule or the Structured Clinical Interview for DSM-III-R. Where interviewers agreed on a diagnosis of GAD after the interviews, correlation coefficients were calculated for reliability of agreement of the patient's symptoms across the three clinics. The answers to two questions about excessive worry were separately examined.

Results: The top symptoms suffered by most patients across the three clinics were irritability, tension fatigue and feeling keyed up. GAD patients reported worry during a significantly higher percentage of the day (59.1%) than non-GAD patients (41.7%). Very few people with GAD said they did not worry excessively about minor matters.

Evaluation: Good agreement between three samples suggests high reliability in the method. The quasi-experimental design is high in validity. The responses to the interviews may have shown desirability bias but they were structured. Debates – 'Is Psychology a Science'? Once again the issue of accurate diagnosis is raised and the use of interview data opens up questions of experimenter effects and possible bias. Ethnocentrism – exactly what is excessive worry and would this be defined similarly everywhere? Usefulness – it helped to find criteria that could discriminate GAD from other anxiety disorders and contributed to increasing the reliability of the DSM-IV diagnostic criteria.

▲ Figure 8.1

Phobia treatments – Behavioural

See page 46 for McGrath's successful behavioural treatment of a noise phobia in a nine-year-old girl using systematic desensitisation.

Phobia treatments – Biological
Liebowitz, M.R. *et al.* (1988)
Pharmacotherapy of social phobia

Aim: To find out if people with a social phobia could be helped by taking either phenelzine or atenolol.

Background: A social phobia is a fear of interacting with other people. Phenelezine prevents the breakdown of the monoamine neurotransmitters serotonin, melatonin, norepinephrine, epinephrine and dopamine. This leads to an increase in the concentrations of these neurochemicals and therefore an alteration in neurochemistry in the brain, making a patient calmer and less depressed. Atenolol is a beta blocker which slows the heart beat and lowers blood pressure.

Sample: 80 patients meeting the DSM-III criteria for social phobia aged 18–50 and who were not suffering from any other medical or psychological condition took part. Only 41 had completed the trial by the time the paper was published.

Method/procedure: Single-blind placebo controlled trial. Patients were given a placebo for seven days to see if they got better. If they did, they were not included in the treatment phase. They were randomised to the three treatments in an independent measures design. Patients were given either phenelzine or matching placebo or atenolol or matching placebo. Eight weeks later they were assessed by independent evaluators and then they continued for a further eight weeks. After 16 weeks half the patients who were recovering got a placebo for four weeks, while the others continued to get the active drugs. Assessment was by blood tests to check they were taking the medication and a series of rating scales.

Results: Phenelzine but not atenolol was effective in the treatment of the phobia by appearing to reduce anticipatory anxiety and the difference appeared by eight weeks.

Evaluation: Small sample size at the time the paper was published. The use of rating scales repeatedly by the patients may increase demand characteristics, although it helps with test-retest reliability and use of several different instruments helps construct validity.

Debates: This is a reductionist explanation of a phobia, reducing it to brain chemistry balance as opposed to a personality disorder. Usefulness – many people have social phobias, so if a drug treatment is available it would perhaps support them until they could master their fear through CBT.

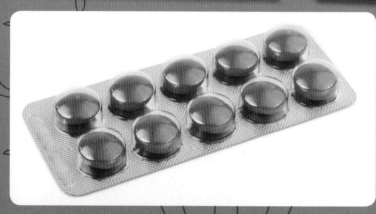

▲ **Figure 8.2** Patients were either given the real drug or a placebo

Phobia treatments – Cognitive

Ost, L.G. and Westling, B. (1995) Applied relaxation vs. cognitive behaviour therapy in the treatment of panic disorder

Aim: To compare cognitive behavioural therapy (CBT) with applied relaxation to treat panic disorder.

Background: The cognitive theory of panic disorders proposes that people who experience panic attacks have a well-developed tendency to interpret body sensations in a catastrophic way. This then leads to a vicious cycle of symptoms and interpretations leading to a panic attack.

Sample: 38 patients who fulfilled the DSM-III criteria for panic disorder, 8 of whom also had mild agoraphobia. They were recruited through referrals from psychiatrists and adverts in the paper and had to have had at least three panic attacks and suffered with the condition for at least a year. 26 were female and 12 male with an average age of 32.6.

Method/procedure: Patients were randomly assigned to the two treatments with assessment pre- and post-treatment and follow-up one year later. Patients completed questionnaires and were interviewed at the start and instructed in what to do if they got a panic attack and how to keep a panic diary. After the last session the patient again filled out a questionnaire and had a brief interview. One year later they were mailed the questionnaire and had a telephone interview. Both treatments were given, lasting one hour, once a week for 12 weeks. Progressive relaxation techniques and the normal CBT approach were used.

Results: CBT patients were 74% panic free after the treatment and 89% panic free after one year. The relaxation patients were 65% panic free immediately after treatment and 82% panic free after one year, so both treatments worked, but CBT was more effective. Both groups reduced their medication to the same extent.

Evaluation: It is impossible to control for any cognitive changes that might have occurred in the relaxation group. Self-reports were used to collect the data so patients could have shown demand characteristics in changing their responses from the first to the second and third questionnaires as it was expected. No control group and the patients were not drug free during the trial.

Debates: Nature/nurture – is there a panicky personality or is this a condition which is nurtured? Usefulness – panic disorder is clearly susceptible to treatment and either method would help a patient reduce medication.

▲ **Figure 8.3** Several of the participants suffered from agoraphobia

EXPLANATIONS AND TREATMENTS OF AN AFFECTIVE DISORDER: DEPRESSION

You are required to choose only ONE disorder (either affective or anxiety or psychotic) and follow it through its explanations and treatments (there is no need to do more). Explanations of an affective disorder are given below.

Depression explanations – Behavioural

Lewisohn et al. (1972) Pleasant events, activity schedules, and depressions

Aim: To compare the amount of positive reinforcement received by depressed and non-depressed patients.

Background: If people lose the positive reinforcement they get from living a normal life involving work, relaxation and friends, they may become depressed. This is often the case with people who are made redundant or who leave the armed forces or retire, as these are all major life changes that mean less contact with other people.

Sample: 30 patients who were diagnosed with either depression, a disorder other than depression and 'normal' controls took part.

Method/procedure: This was a quasi-experiment with an independent measures design. It was a longitudinal study over 30 days where participants completed a self-report of pleasant activities on the Pleasant Events Schedule. Participants scored 0 = Never, 1 = Sometimes or 2 = Often for how often they experienced a pleasant event and 0, 1 or 2 for how much they enjoyed it. They also completed a self-rating of depression using the Depression Adjective Checklist.

▼ **Table 8.1** Example items on the Pleasant Events Schedule (there are 320 in all)

Being in the country	Wearing expensive clothes
Watching sport	Going to a rock concert
Giving to charity	Meeting someone new of the opposite sex
Going to the beach	Going naked
Getting drunk	

▲ **Figure 8.4** Being in the country is one of the items on the Pleasant Events Schedule

Results: There were significant positive correlations between mood ratings and pleasant activities, with involvement in more pleasant activities being correlated with more positive mood ratings. However, the correlations varied from 0 to –0.66, which shows great individual differences and the likelihood of other factors than positive reinforcement at work in depression.

Evaluation: Working through 320 items twice may have been trying for the participants, who had only a choice of three scores to give to each item.

Debates: Individual vs. situational explanations of behaviour. The large number of individual differences suggests a strong element of an individual explanation of this behaviour. Free will vs. determinism – this study suggests that a good mood is determined by positive reinforcement. Reductionism vs. holism – reducing the change in mood to a loss of positive reinforcement ignores the complexity of all the factors which could have created a depression.

Usefulness: This has limited usefulness when there is so much individual variation, despite the quite strong correlation. However, it shows that having positive experiences in life are really important and are linked to good mental health.

Depression explanations – Biological

Sullivan, P.F. *et al.* (2000) Genetic epidemiology of major depression: review and meta-analysis

Aim: To discover to what extent major depression runs in families and what are the relative contributions of genes and environment in the origins of the disorder.

Background: Major depression has been projected to become the second leading cause of disability worldwide by 2020 (second to ischemic heart disease). There are many primary studies of the genetic epidemiology of major depression. However, no single source had provided a summation of these data, which have been gathered by many teams of researchers worldwide over the past three decades.

Sample: 5 family studies, 3 adoption studies and 5 twin studies were included.

Method/procedure: The authors searched MEDLINE and the reference lists of previous review articles to identify relevant primary studies. The specific inclusion criteria were a clear distinction between bipolar and major depression, blinded assessors at the post treatment phases of the studies and the use of control groups. Some adoption studies were only used for qualitative data. A statistical analysis which calculated the odds of a relation with major depression having a first degree relative with the same disorder were calculated with the data from the studies.

Results: The odds ratios for subjects with major depression versus first-degree relative status were similar across the five studies at 2.84. The results of two of the three adoption reports were consistent with genetic influences on liability to major depression. Results from the five twin studies suggested that familial depression had a heritability rate of 31–42% with a 5% contribution of environmental effects common to siblings within the home. The conclusion is that major depression does run in families and its transmission mostly or entirely results from genetic influences.

Evaluation: This was a rigorous sampling method which covered many hundreds of patients worldwide, so very generalisable and reliable findings. The final percentage of heritability for depression at around 30–40% contrasts with 70% for schizophrenia. It leaves a lot of room for environmental factors such as stress and life events.

Debates: Nature/ nurture: this paper puts forward a classic argument of heritability. Usefulness – these findings could lead to screening families as a preventative measure. It moves research closer to understanding the cause of depression, although in itself does not answer that question.

▲ **Figure 8.5** Sullivan *et al.*'s study looked at whether there was a genetic component to depression

Depression explanations – Cognitive

Beck's Cognitive theory of depression is on page 45 and looks at depression as a series of illogical and distorted thinking. This theory is applicable here.

Depression treatments – Behavioural
Lewisohn, P.M. *et al.* (1990) Cognitive behavioural treatment for depressed adolescents

Aim: To test whether the Coping with Depression (CWD) course would work with a sample of adolescents.

Background: The behavioural model of depression, as suggested by Lewisohn in 1979, suggests that depression can result from a stressor which disrupts normal behaviour patterns, causing a low rate of positive reinforcement. The CWD course was derived from this theoretical perspective. It was designed to teach people techniques and strategies to cope with the problems related to their depression. These strategies include improving social skills, addressing depressogenic thinking, increasing pleasant activities and relaxation training. Inevitably, some of this training affects cognitive processes and so the therapy is really cognitive behavioural.

Sample: 59 patients aged 14–18 were recruited by letter to doctors and schools and announcements made in the media. They met the DSM-III diagnosis of a major depressive disorder but could not have any other complications or be actively suicidal. They had to stop all other medication to take part.

Method/procedure: A longitudinal, randomised controlled trial with an independent measures design of three conditions: 1. adolescent only, 2. adolescent and parent and 3. waiting list control. The adolescent only group received the CWD course for 14 two-hour sessions twice a week for seven weeks. The identical course was given to the adolescents in the parent and adolescent group combined with seven two-hour sessions once a week for the parents only. The goal for the parents was to learn how to reinforce their children positively and learn coping skills to reduce tension at home. The waiting list group served to control for time and the assessments and they were told they might have to wait for treatment. (If they needed to, they could withdraw and get treatment.) Checks were made on the standard of treatment across conditions and depression was measured with the usual rating scales such as the BDI, pre- and post-treatment.

Results: Approximately 52% of the adolescent and parent group and 57% of the adolescent only teens still met the diagnostic criteria for depression, with very little change in the waiting list controls with 95% still being depressed. This was still maintained at the two-year follow-up interviews for the 50% of the sample still remaining.

Evaluation: It would have been good to have a medication-only group as a comparison. These parents cared enough to go to treatment which might be unrepresentative over a larger population. Method is well controlled and replicable.

Debates: Freewill vs. determinism – the use of the parents is interesting here. Could they be a factor in determining the success of the treatment because they were part of the cause of the depression? Usefulness – the study shows promising results for the CWD course and for positive reinforcement.

Depression treatments – Biological
See Karp and Frank on page 46 which looks at the biological approach to medicating patients with depression.

Depression Treatments - Cognitive

Lam, D.H. *et al.* (2003) on page 47 could be used here, although it uses bipolar disorder and not major depression. An alternative study is by Strunk, D.R. *et al.* (2010) (see below).

Strunk, D.R. *et.al.* (2010) The process of change in cognitive therapy for depression: predictors of early inter-session symptom gains

Aim: To compare cognitive and behavioural treatments for depression.

Background: As described previously, cognitive therapy is based on the work of Beck and attempts to change the illogical thoughts which lead to negative behaviours and emotions leading to depression.

Sample: The study involved 60 patients who were diagnosed with mild to moderate major depression and who were being treated at two university clinics. All the patients were being treated by one of six cognitive therapists and agreed to have their therapy sessions videotaped for study.

Method/procedure: A comparative study with an independent measures design. The study focused on the first few weeks of therapy because other studies suggest that is when patients make the largest improvement in depression levels. Two trained raters reviewed videotapes of five therapy sessions for each patient. Six therapists took the sessions. They rated how much therapists relied on cognitive and behavioural methods and other aspects of the sessions. In addition, patients completed a questionnaire at each session that measured their depression levels. The researchers examined the relationship between specific techniques used by their therapists and the extent of improvement in patients' depression scores from one session to the next.

Results: Results showed that patients' depression scores improved significantly when their therapists focused on cognitive techniques, but did not change when their therapists focused on behavioural techniques. Patients also improved more when they collaborated with their therapists about a plan for treatment and followed that plan. Unsurprisingly, patients also showed greater improvement when they were more engaged in the therapy process and were open to suggestions from their therapist.

Evaluation: How was quality of the therapist controlled? This is a major confounding variable. Data collected by scores on depression scales have the usual issues of accuracy and reliability. Would someone with more severe depression respond in the same way?

Debates: Free will vs. determinism – the change in thinking achieved through cognitive therapy suggests there is an element of free will over how you interpret your mood. Depression is not all determined by outside pressures. Usefulness – these are very useful results which show that talking therapies are very effective for tackling depression. They also suggest that patients ought to be fully involved in their treatments.

◄ **Figure 8.6** Outcomes were better when patients were involved in drawing up their own treatment plan

EXPLANATIONS AND TREATMENTS OF A PSYCHOTIC DISORDER: SCHIZOPHRENIA

You are required to choose only ONE disorder (either affective or anxiety or psychotic) and follow it through its explanations and treatments (there is no need to do more). Explanations of a psychotic disorder are given below.

Schizophrenia explanations – Behavioural

Liberman, R.P. (1982) Assessment of social skills

Aim: To assess the extent to which schizophrenic patients lack social skills and to propose that social skill training should be a part of treatment.

Background: Schizophrenic patients often have difficulty with social skills such as meeting and greeting, making eye contact, making conversation and expressing feelings. There are two types of communication: *instrumental* which means communication with a goal, such as buying something in a shop, and *social-emotional* communication, such as asking someone how they feel.

Sample: Lots of pieces of research and case studies which looked at patients with psychotic illnesses are reviewed in the article.

Method/procedure: This was a review article which analysed the social skills of psychotic patients in three categories: 1. Their *topographical* social skills, which includes verbal and non-verbal elements of communication; 2. a *functional* view of their social skills, which is about using communication to achieve a goal such as returning a defective item of clothes; 3. an *information processing* view of their social skills, which includes the correct recognition of gestures and postures as expressions of thoughts and feelings. Methods of assessment were self-report, interview, role-play tests, naturalistic interactions and tangible evidence of completion of a task such as a ticket stub or job application.

Results: On all measures schizophrenic patients had difficulty. Institutionalisation led to loss of skills and faulty cognition meant they misinterpreted other people's meanings. A new finding was that they had difficulty with attention, perception and information processing. A lack of social skills led to a lack of positive reinforcement in their lives which in turn led to social withdrawal.

Evaluation: Schizophrenic patients found filling out self-reports confusing and role-plays lack external validity and are beset by demand characteristics. The naturalistic interactions which are staged with stooges are possibly unethical as they involve deception.

Debates: This is a fairly reductionist approach although many different forms of communication difficulty are examined. Usefulness – this is very useful research which can be used to formulate training programmes for psychotic patients.

Schizophrenia explanations – Biological
Gottesman, I.J. & Shields, J. (1976)
A critical review of recent adoption, twin and family studies of schizophrenia: behavioural genetics perspectives

Summary of results: All three adoption studies showed increased incidence of schizophrenia in adopted children with a schizophrenic biological parent, but normal children fostered with a schizophrenic parent did not develop schizophrenia. In one study, the biological siblings of children with schizophrenia were found to have a 19.2% chance of also developing the condition. The twin studies also supported the biological explanation with monozygotic twins showing a 58% concordance rate compared to 12% in dizygotic twins.

Schizophrenia explanations – Cognitive
Maher, B.A. (1988) Anomalous experiences and delusional thinking

Aim: To develop a model to explain why some schizophrenic patients experience the positive symptoms of delusions and hearing voices.

Background: Recent research has sought to explain the mechanisms of the formation of delusions in more detail. The present model from King's College London suggests that delusions are formed as shown in Figure 8.7.

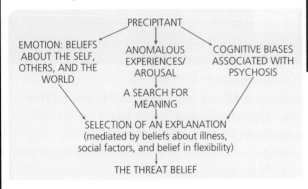

▲ **Figure 8.7** Summary of the formation of a persecutory delusion (source: Freeman, *et al.*, 2002)

Explanation of the formation of delusions: The emergence of symptoms comes from an interaction between vulnerability from genes, biological, psychological and social factors and stress. Therefore the formation of the delusion will begin with a precipitator such as a life-stress event or drug misuse. This causes arousal which creates an inner-outer confusion causing a strange experience, e.g. thoughts being experienced as voices, actions being explained as unintended or more subtle cognitive experiences

Evaluation: There is a lot of evidence that it is socially anxious individuals with low self-esteem who are more likely to develop psychosis. Research needs to be done on exploring the types of explanations that patients have for their experiences to provide further support for the model.

Debates: Nature/nurture interactions are very much a part of this model. Is this a state or trait explanation? Usefulness – the beliefs are maintained because they provide the relief of an explanation for the patient of his strange experiences so this can lead to a line of therapy where alternative meanings for the delusions can be explored with the patient.

▲ **Figure 8.8**

such as perceptual anomalies, which in turn drive a search for meaning (Maher, 1988).

In the search for meaning, pre-existing beliefs are drawn upon, so if a person already has a negative self-image or belief that the world is hostile then they will tend to form persecutory delusions. The explanations considered in the search for meaning will be influenced by cognitive biases associated with psychosis including the 'jumping to conclusions' bias, which may limit the amount of data gathered by the patient to support a conclusion. Other biases include Theory of Mind (Frith, 1992) and a tendency to blame others and misinterpreting the intentions and behaviour of others.

Put simply, patients have to make a choice between something being wrong with them (e.g. they are going mad) or that something is wrong with the world. Believing they are going mad is more distressing than believing that they are being persecuted and so a persecution belief is created.

Treatments – Behavioural

Paul, G.L. and Lentz, R.J. (1977) Psychosocial treatment of chronic mental patients

Aim: To compare social learning against milieu therapy for treating patients with psychotic disorders.

Background: Paul and Lenz believed that positive reinforcement techniques could selectively reinforce socially acceptable behaviours and reduce unacceptable behaviour based on a token economy program. A therapeutic milieu is a structured group setting in which positive peer pressure, trust, safety and repetition of behaviours needing to be improved provides the setting for group members to work through their psychological issues.

Sample: 84 chronically institutionalised, psychotic patients from four state hospitals in Illinois took part.

Method/procedure: This was a field experiment with an independent measures design. Patients were put into three groups: one was the social learning group, one the milieu therapy group and the control group, who remained in hospital for the usual therapy. The social learning therapy group followed a token economy system with rewards over approximately 85% of their available time and this was matched by a similar time spent in milieu therapy by the second group. The social learning group would be rewarded for behaviours which would increase their ability to function outside the institution, such as personal care, making conversation and managing other daily tasks. The control condition was varied but generally spent less time in any kind of structured program of treatment which only occupied approximately 5% of their time.

Results: By the end of the study, 92.5% of the behaviour group, 71% of the milieu group and 48% of the control group were released. This clear difference emerged at every assessment which was done with a battery of psychometric tests.
The results support the use of token economies in institutions to help prepare patients for release into the community.

Evaluation: Good internal and external validity because of the design being a field experiment. Good control of amount of time in therapy.

Debates: Determinism vs. free will – supports the behaviourist view that behaviour is a result of external positive and negative reinforcers. Usefulness – these are very useful findings which can easily be put into effect in many similar institutions and which are easy to train people to implement.

Results: Of the 17 patients receiving the placebo, seven relapsed after a mean of 19 weeks and 7 out of 11 drug treated patients dropped out after a mean of 21 weeks. Therefore only three patients completed the study. Among the 11 drug treated patients there were no relapses but two dropped out at four weeks and one at 24 weeks due to toxic side effects that meant they had to stop taking the medication. Therefore although drug treatment appears to work, it cannot be tolerated by quite large percentages of patients.

Treatments – Biological

Kane, J.M. et al. (1982) Fluphenazine vs. placebo in patients with remitted acute first-episode schizophrenia

Aim: To compare the effectiveness of fluphenazine against a placebo.

Background: Drug treatments are a big part of the treatment of schizophrenia and the fact that they appear to reduce symptoms suggests that there is an underlying biological cause or reaction in the brain. Patients with an acute first attack of schizophrenia are thought to have the best chance of remission and there is a debate as to whether using drugs is a good idea or not at the point when patients are no longer experiencing symptoms. This study investigates patients in this phase of the illness.

Sample: 28 patients who had recently recovered from an acute-onset first episode schizophrenic illness took part.

Treatments – Cognitive

Sensky, T. *et al.* (2000) A randomised controlled trial of cognitive behavioural therapy for persistent symptoms in schizophrenia resistant to medication

Aim: To compare cognitive behavioural therapy with a befriending control for treatment of schizophrenia.

Background: Research evidence supports the effectiveness for cognitive behavioural therapy in the treatment of schizophrenia where, if the positive symptoms are the result of distorted perceptions, it should be possible to alter those perceptions.

Sample: 90 patients from five clinical areas, aged 16–60, who had the symptoms of schizophrenia for at least six months and who adhered to their drug medication (chlorpromazine) but who had not shown great improvement.

Method/procedure: A randomised controlled design was used. Both treatments were given by two experienced nurses. Patients were assessed at baseline, after treatment over nine months and at a nine-month follow-up with a battery of psychometric tests including the Comprehensive Psychiatric Rating scale (CPRS). The assessments were rated by people who were blind to the conditions. CBT followed the usual pattern of identifying problem behaviours, finding the antecedents and developing a normalising strategy. Any depression was also treated. The befriending group controlled for contact time (45 minutes per week) and focused on neutral topics such as hobbies and sports with no direct intervention on symptoms.

Results: Both the CBT and befriending groups improved and at the end of the treatment there was no significant difference between them. However, nine months later the CBT group showed significant gains across all the measures, suggesting that it was a superior form of treatment with lasting benefit.

Evaluation: There was a good spread of the sample across different regions. However, this group are traditionally the easiest to treat and they were all good adherers to medical advice. A wider sample may not show the same differences.

It could be that the drugs were just taking longer to work.

Debates: Psychology as a science – this study is a good example with its strong methodology and sampling. Free-will vs. determinism – the research suggests that we can take control of mental illness with CBT. Usefulness – CBT is helpful in treating both positive and negative symptoms of schizophrenia. This is really important because the negative symptoms are very hard to treat.

Method/procedure: This was a one-year double-blind comparison of fluphenazine and placebo. Patients were randomly assigned to the three groups and given drugs or placebo. Patients were removed if they dropped out, had bad side effects or relapsed.

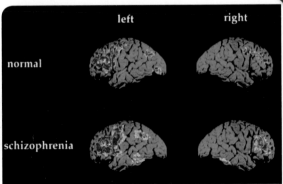

▲ **Figure 8.9** A schizophrenic brain scan compared to a normal brain scan

Evaluation: This research suggests that drugs are effective in preventing relapses and the findings come from a strongly controlled double-blind trial which is high in validity and reliability.

Debates: Psychology as a science – this is the best kind of well-controlled scientific method. It is a **reductionist** explanation of schizophrenia which looks for a chemical explanation of the symptoms. Usefulness – this was a very small sample and the problems with tolerating the drug may limit its usefulness for many patients.

SPORT AND EXERCISE PSYCHOLOGY

9. Sport and the individual (see pp. 64–69)

Is a certain personality type likely to be more successful in sport? Does sport allow the healthy release of aggression or does it stimulate aggressive responses? How important is motivation to successful sport performance?

1. **Personality:** outlines Cattell's 16 personality factor (16PF) questionnaire, much used in sporting contexts as an assessment tool. Eysenck's trait theory of personality and its proposed biological bases is presented, as well as the main dimensions of extrovert-introvert (E) and neurotic-stable (N). Finally the personality profiles of four different athletic groups (football, wrestling, gymnasts, karate) are assessed using the 16PF and then compared.

2. **Aggression:** covers Freud's 'instinct' theory of aggression (which he considered innate). 'Cue' theory proposes that environmental stimuli may enhance or inhibit aggression. Bandura's Social Learning Theory (SLT) considers whether we learn aggression in a variety of social contexts, e.g. sport.

3. **Motivation:** outlines the concept of achievement motivation and suggests those with a high need to achieve (n-Ach) do better in sport. The development of a multi-dimensional measure of sport-specific motivation, the SOQ (Sport Orientation Questionnaire) is outlined, including its validation. Finally, self-determination theory, the basic needs involved in self-determination, and the role of intrinsic and extrinsic motivation is considered.

10. Sport performance (see pp. 70–75)

Do arousal and anxiety affect sporting performance positively or negatively? What are the roles of self-efficacy and confidence in sporting performance?

1. **Arousal:** starts with the classic 'dancing mice' study investigating the effect of arousal (mild electrical stimulation) on learning. Lacey's distinction of different types of arousal (electro-cortical, autonomic and behavioural) is useful for coaches to learn to identify signs which might indicate over-arousal (and the likelihood of negative effects on performance). Oxendine summarises reviewed research which has investigated the effects of arousal on performance.

2. **Anxiety:** Marten's early Sport Competition Anxiety Test (SCAT), measuring trait anxiety is considered more valid and reliable as it was developed in a sporting context. However, the later development of the Competitive State Anxiety Inventory-2 (CSAI-2) acknowledges the need for a multi-dimensional measure (cognitive and somatic anxiety and self-confidence). Fazey & Hardy's catastrophe theory presents a more realistic picture of what can happen to an athlete's performance when they have both high cognitive anxiety and physiological arousal.

3. **Self-confidence:** believed to be the crucial difference between successful and unsuccessful athletes. Bandura's theory of self-efficacy has proved useful, with the four sources of efficacy expectations indicating practical ways of supporting athletes. Vealey's sport-specific model of self-confidence allows for continual development/response to performance and Wood's four functions of imagery are outlined.

11. Social psychology of sport (see pp. 76–81)

Does being in a sporting group influence sporting performance positively or negatively? Are the effects of being watched likely to enhance or damage sporting performance? Can leadership and coaching make a difference to sporting performance?

1. **Group cohesion:** outlines Tuckman's developmental sequence in small groups, which arising out of a literature review has, nonetheless, been useful in sporting contexts. The effect on performance of others is considered in Latane's social loafing experiment (a conceptual replication of Ringlemann's early rope-pulling study). Carron's model for developing cohesiveness in sports teams takes into account a wide range of factors and makes the important distinction between task and social cohesion.

2. **Audience effects:** Cottrell considers 'mere presence' is insufficient to stimulate performance. Zajonc's investigation into social enhancement or impairment of performance in cockroaches does make a sound 'theoretical' point and illustrates interesting design/control features. Home advantage in four sports is investigated (football, baseball, hockey, basketball).

3. **Leadership and coaching:** Stogdill's search into personal factors associated with leadership is an heroic summary of 124 studies, but rather inconclusive. A multi-dimensional model of leadership moves away from traits to consider leader behaviours/styles and the effectiveness of training coaches is substantiated in the context of young baseball players.

12. Exercise psychology (see pp. 82-87)

What are the benefits of exercise on both physiological and psychological health? Can exercise ever be 'bad' for you?

1. **Exercise and pathology:** the benefits of physical exercise are investigated and confirmed in a study of women newly diagnosed with breast cancer. A study involving HIV diagnosed patients also reports positive benefits (on mood, life satisfaction and physical self-efficacy) which we have to infer will impact on immune system functioning. The possible negative effects of exercise are lastly considered, e.g. trying to maintain low weight/slim physique, which puts individuals at risk of developing eating disorders.

2. **Exercise and mental health:** endorphins which are released during sustained exercise are known to make people feel good and this first study outlines what research has confirmed about the endorphin hypothesis. A review investigating the effects of exercise on mental health essentially confirms the positive benefits. The mental health model tries to move us from pure description to prediction of success in sport and the measure used, POMS (Profile of Mood States), has shown predictive value.

3. **Issues:** the first study investigates different training schedules and their effect on performance which challenges the notion that lots of exercise must necessarily be good for you. A measure for Social Physique Anxiety is developed and evaluated and a study of weight lifters investigates the power of expectancy effects on performance improvements with the ethically challenging notion of taking anabolic steroids (in fact a placebo).

PERSONALITY

Cattell, R.B. (1956) The scientific analysis of personality

Background: Allport and Odbert (1936) reviewed dictionaries to identify personality-related words/ adjectives. They found c. 18,000 which they condensed to c. 4,500 personality descriptors which were considered to be observable and relatively permanent traits.

Aim: To identify personality traits that would allow personality assessment.

Method/procedure: Cattell analysed the Allport and Odbert condensed list, organised it into 181 clusters and then asked participants to rate people they knew using the adjectives. Factor analysis resulted in the generation of 12 factors; Cattell added four more he thought should be included, resulting in his 16PF (personality factors) questionnaire. Participants' responses were quantitative, i.e. number on a scale.

Examples/descriptions of some of Cattell's personality factor scales:

Q4 (tension) ranges from 'relaxed, composed, low drive' to 'tense, restless, high drive'.

Q3 (perfectionism) ranges from 'undisciplined, impulsive' to 'controlled, compulsive'.

H (social boldness) ranges from 'shy, timid, threat sensitive' to 'socially bold/unafraid'.

A (warmth) ranges from 'reserved, cool' to 'warm, easygoing, likes people'.

E (dominance) ranges from 'submissive, accommodating' to 'dominant, assertive, opinionated'.

Q2 (self-reliance) ranges from 'group orientated, sociable' to 'self-sufficient, resourceful, self-directed'.

G (rules consciousness) ranges from 'expedient, disregards rules' to 'conforming, persevering, rule-bound'.

Evaluation: Cattell himself admitted that mood, motivation and situation could influence responses on the 16PF which means individuals will not necessarily show similar scores each time they complete it. Therefore reliability can be questioned. Socially desirable responses means validity can be questioned. Possible researcher bias (Cattell added four more factors).

Debates: Individual explanations of behaviour. Reductionism – does not take into account influence of situations/social factors. Usefulness – despite validity and reliability questions Cattell's 16PF is recognised and well used, particularly within sporting contexts.

Link: AS study, Rosenhan – dangers of labelling/self-fulfilling prophecy.

Eysenck, H.J. (1965) Trait theory

Background: Eysenck's trait theory developed essentially from studying monozygotic (MZ, identical) and dizygotic (DZ, non-identical) twins.

Theory: Originally, Eysenck proposed two dimensions to personality, E (ranging from extrovert to introvert) and N (ranging from neurotic to stable).

Eysenck later (1975) added a third dimension (P) – psychoticism (seen to identify aggression/mental instability). These dimensions were arrived at by use of factor analysis. Eysenck theorises there is a biological basis for personality.

E: The Reticular Activating System (RAS) monitors cortical arousal levels. An individual with low levels of cortical arousal (or under-arousal) is bored and therefore seeks stimulation (i.e. an extrovert); while an individual with high levels of cortical arousal (over-arousal) prefers quiet and calm (i.e. an introvert).

N: The Autonomic Nervous System (ANS) responds to emotion-producing stimuli. Someone who shows a strong/immediate reaction to stressful (emotion-producing) stimuli (a low anxiety threshold) is neurotic, i.e. scores high on the (N) scale; while someone who is stable (high anxiety threshold) reacts more calmly to minor stressors, i.e. scores low on the (N) scale.

P: Associated with the hormonal system, e.g. testosterone (high levels linked with aggression). A low score on (P) indicates someone who is empathic and cooperative, while a high score on (P) indicates someone who is egocentric, aggressive, non-conformist, cold, impulsive and hostile. (Interestingly some of these qualities/characteristics are necessary, even rewarded, in sport, e.g. aggression.)

Eysenck devised a questionnaire to test individuals on these dimensions called the EPQ (Eysenck Personality Questionnaire, 1975). Participants respond 'yes/no' to a series of questions.

An example of an item (question) from each scale follows.

E – Are you rather lively?

N – Do you worry about awful things that might happen?

P – Would it upset you a lot to see a child suffer?

Kroll, W. and Crenshaw, W. (1970) Personality profile analysis of four athletic groups

Background: Some common beliefs about sport and personality: 1. certain characteristics are necessary for successful performance; 2. these will vary with specific sport.

Aim: To make between-sport comparisons, using Cattell's 16PF on groups at regional or national level in a variety of sports.

Sample/participants: 387 (with high-level skills in sport). 81 footballers (college players, mid-USA); 141 gymnasts (14 college/ university teams, national cross-section of USA); 94 amateur wrestlers (Olympic team and national tournament winners); 71 karate participants (five teams, south-western USA).

Method/procedure: Independent measures using a questionnaire. Cattell's 16PF, form A, administered and a 15-item lie scale of the MMPI (those scoring seven or more on the lie scale were removed from study, since validity is in question). Data analysed statistically by multi-variate profile analysis (on whole personality profile, not individual factors).

Results: Significant differences (at 1% level) between all groups were found, except between footballers and wrestlers, i.e. their personality profiles were similar. Footballers and wrestlers differ significantly from gymnasts and karate participants. Gymnasts scored lowest of all groups on Q4 (i.e. were most relaxed) while karate scored highest (i.e. were most tense).

▼ **Table 9.1** Summary of some differences identified between groups

Comparison groups	Differences identified (factors and description)
Footballers – Wrestlers	
Footballers – Karate	Q2 – Footballers more group-oriented/dependent, while Karate more self-sufficient
Footballers – Gymnasts	H – Gymnasts more adventurous/ socially bold than footballers Q2 – Footballers more group-oriented/dependent, gymnasts more self-sufficient;
Wrestlers – Gymnasts	H – Gymnasts more adventurous/ socially bold than wrestlers
Gymnasts – Karate	Q4 – Gymnasts more relaxed than karate; G – gymnasts more expedient, disregard rules, karate more conscientious and rule-bound
Wrestlers – Karate	Q2 – Wrestlers more group-oriented/dependent, karate more self-sufficient; Q4 – Wrestlers more relaxed, karate more tense G – Wrestlers more expedient, disregard rules, karate more conscientious and rule-bound

Evaluation: Use of lie-scale improves validity. Fairly large sample in each sport is reliable, however, cannot necessarily generalise findings across wider age-range, gender, skill/fitness level.

Debates: Nature/nurture – cannot conclude whether individuals with different personalities choose different sports or whether participating in sport over time changes personality, therefore question usefulness (also as does not necessarily distinguish individual versus team players); however useful to identify individuals with high Q4 (tension) scores. Reductionist – does not take into account other factors, e.g. the effect of life experiences/upbringing on development of personality.

Evaluation: The proposition of a biological basis for his personality theory is a strength. In addition the EPQ incorporates a lie scale to establish validity of responses. The validity of the (N) scale was tested when Eysenck had individuals diagnosed as neurotic completing this scale and they scored high.
Debates: Individual explanations of behaviour/nature. Usefulness – to assess suitability of players for position of team captain, coaches might look for high (E) scores and low (N) scores.

AGGRESSION

Freud, S. (1901) Theory of aggression

Background: Ethological research (studying animals in their natural environment) argues that aggression is innate (Lorenz, 1966) as it is present in all species. It has survival value: involved in fighting to gain reproductive access to a mate, protecting territory and/or to achieve dominance in a group.

Psychoanalytic theory: Freud also considered aggression as innate, arising out of what he considered are our death instincts – destructive – which he called thanatos. These are in conflict with our life instincts – sexually driven, positive and creative – which he called eros. Freud considered that to maintain psychological health we have to manage our aggression and allow its release – a process called **catharcism**. Sport can allow the release of aggression and is therefore considered to be cathartic. If aggression is not managed the likelihood is that pent-up energy will 'explode'. Another way of understanding how humans 'manage' aggression is by referring to one of Freud's ego-defences, displacement. For example, if someone makes you angry/frustrated but you are unable to communicate this to them (e.g. your boss, your parents) you might release pent-up anger by re-directing (displacing) it onto another, more acceptable (available), target, e.g. a friend (this can be with or without a legitimate trigger). You might also displace your aggression onto an object (e.g. using a punch bag) or achieve release through effort in exercise.

Evaluation: Engaging in sport should lead to reduced levels of aggression (according to both Freud and Ethological theory); however, this is challenged by cue theory (see below).

Debates: Biological determinism (of innate drives) does not take into account free will. Reductionist – does not take into account social factors/situational explanations/cultural norms. Usefulness: theories are not generally considered very useful unless they have been tested and research upholds their claims.

Berkowitz, L. and Geen, R. (1966) Film violence and the cue properties of available targets

Background: Long-running debate about whether viewing violence is likely to lead to imitation/increased violence.

Aim: To test the eliciting-cue hypothesis (i.e. whether cues in the environment which can be interpreted as either aggressive or non-aggressive and elicit or inhibit aggressive responses).

Sample/participants: 88 male Wisconsin university students (72 volunteers from introductory psychology class to gain course credits; 16 recruited from an introductory sociology class).

Method/procedure: Laboratory experiment (2 x 2 x 2 factorial design). IVs – a) angered/non-angered condition; b) confederate introduced as either Kirk or Bob; c) aggressive film/non-aggressive film viewed; d) name mediated association, or not. Participants told experiments involved giving/receiving mild electric shocks and given opportunity to withdraw, then given a problem-solving task which was evaluated by peer (confederate) and feedback given to participant via mild electric shocks to arm (1–10), i.e. the poorer evaluation delivering more shocks (either received 1 or 7, for 'non-angered' or 'angered' conditions). Participant confirmed number of shocks received and then completed a brief questionnaire rating moods on four scales. Next the participant and confederate viewed a film, either 'aggressive' (fight scene from *Champion* with Kirk as main character) or 'non-aggressive' (track race of two men running a mile in under four minutes) and with attention drawn to same name (Kirk) as confederate or not. Next, peer (confederate) sent to complete problem-solving task which participant evaluated and delivered feedback via shocks (1–10). Participant was given final questionnaire about how much he liked his peer (confederate) and then debriefed about deception.

Results: Participants tested to check memory of their peer's name (all 88 remembered) and all correctly reported the number of shocks received.

1. *Mood ratings:* 'Angered' participants (who received seven shocks) reported feeling more angry than 'non-angered' (received one shock).

2. *Liking of peer (confederate):* 'Angered' participants expressed a lower preference for peer as a partner in any subsequent experiment (+ two other lower preferences expressed) than 'non-angered'.

3. *Name-mediated association:* confederates with aggressive link (i.e. Kirk) received a significantly higher number of shocks than Bob.

The greatest number of aggressive responses (shocks delivered to confederate) given by 'angered' condition participants, who had seen 'aggressive' film, with peer named Kirk (attention drawn to same name as protagonist).

Bandura, A. *et al.* (1963) Social learning theory

Background: An early theory about aggression proposed that frustration is a necessary condition for aggression to be displayed (frustration-aggression, Dollard *et al.*, 1939). Social learning theory (SLT) is seen as arising/developing out of behaviourism (which explains behaviour as a consequence of observation, imitation and reinforcement). SLT explains behaviour is acquired as a result of experience with others (rather than acquired alone), i.e. being driven/determined by the situation/social context of an individual (rather than being innate, or being driven by unconscious drives or biological predispositions). SLT acknowledges also that reinforcement is not always necessary for learning to take place, although behaviour is more likely to be imitated/learned where positive reinforcement is present (e.g. praise, rewards) and/or where the model has some status or power (e.g. parents, celebrity, etc.), or is similar to us. In addition, SLT acknowledges the importance of cognitions as part of the learning process (i.e. does not see behaviour as simple learned responses to stimuli) and considers that aggression in sport is learned. Observational learning is important in learning skills in sporting contexts; however, sport may be seen as promoting aggression as many sports involve aggressive displays (e.g. martial arts, rugby, boxing, football).

Evaluation: Theory is less reductionist in that it takes into account social, cognitive and learning influences upon the development of behaviour. However, it takes no account of any innate behaviours or biological factors (e.g. high levels of testosterone).

Debates: Nurture – aggression is learned. Reductionism (see above). Useful – it can explain a shy withdrawn youngster (e.g. in an academic context) being confident in a sports setting (and also more useful as it is less reductionist).

Exam tip

Ensure you can define aggression, i.e. it is a behaviour (not just a thought); one that includes intent to harm (a living being); can be verbal (threat) or physical.

Also distinguish **hostile** aggression and **instrumental** aggression. Contrasting viewpoints: sport allows healthy release of aggressive urges OR sport encourages aggression. Link: anger management programmes (forensic treatment programmes) and AS study, Bandura et al.

Evaluation: Good use of controls to allow high confidence in results. Fairly large sample although effectively small number in each condition means reliability can be questioned. All male student sample means we cannot generalise findings.

Debates: Social determinism/situational explanations of behaviour/nurture (aggressive cues/people). Reductionist – does not take into account mental health issues where an aggressive cue may not be required. Usefulness – for sporting events organisers who can eliminate aggressive cues/promote non-aggressive cues (e.g. fluffy mascots behaving in a friendly way).

▲ **Figure 9.1**
Do some sports promote aggression?

MOTIVATION

McClelland, D.C. *et al.* (1953) The Achievement Motive

Background: Earlier research had investigated motivation in relation to physiological needs (food, water, sex; e.g. Hull, 1951). However, this limited view is not useful for sport. McClelland *et al.* engaged in a number of research projects on achievement motivation conducted (mainly) at Wesleyan University, USA, between 1947 and 1953 and this work was published in a book. Individuals can essentially be classified as one of two main personality types: 1. those with a need to achieve (n-Ach) and 2. those with a need to avoid failure (nAF).

1. *High n-Ach*: aim to perform at a high level; persist for longer; value feedback to monitor progress and make improvements/adjustments to performance; like to work alone or with others who have similarly high motivation to achieve; attribute their success/performance to *internal* factors (e.g. effort, determination, concentration).

2. *High n-AF*: may avoid situations/tasks where they are a) likely to be evaluated; b) likely to fail; like to work in groups where their performance may be less noticeable (and where responsibility for any failure can be 'shared' or can be apportioned to another); attribute their success/performance to *external* factors (e.g. luck), their failures to a 'bad referee', opponents 'cheating' etc.

Those with high n-Ach would prefer playing opponents who are 'equal' or 'slightly better' (beating weak opposition is not very satisfying) while those with high n-AF would prefer playing against either weaker opponents (greater chance of winning) or very strong opponents (as blame for failure would be minimal).

Method/procedure: research summarised outlines experimental work where motivation was measured by content analysis. For example, participants were given pictures and their task was to write stories with responses guided by specific questions. A scoring system was designed and clearly identified criteria for content analysis allowed inter-rater reliability to be established.

Debates: Individual explanations of behaviour (n-Ach, n-AF). Reductionist – does not take into account a range of other factors e.g. situational/social, rewards/reinforcement. Usefulness: being able to identify those with high (n-Ach) useful for coaches. Link: attribution theory, locus of control.

Gill, D.L. and Deeter, T.E. (1988) Development of the Sport Orientation Questionnaire (SOQ)

Aim: To develop a (valid and reliable) multi-dimensional measure of sport-specific achievement motivation.

Sample/participants: Three samples recruited:

1. 237 undergraduates enrolled in physical activity skills classes in the fall of 1984 selectively sampled to include both competitive (33 males, 64 females) and non-competitive (40 males, 100 females).

2. 281 undergraduates, selected competitive (77 males, 33 females) and non-competitive (24 males, 84 females).

3. 266 high school students (across grades 9, 10, 11 and 12); 126 competitive sports participants (77 males, 49 females) and 140 non-participants in sport (47 males, 93 females).

Method/procedure: Participants in all three samples completed both the SOQ and the Work and Family Orientation Questionnaire (WOFO – which was included as a general achievement orientation comparison for the SOQ). SOQ items were developed from: 1. reviewing achievement and sport competition literature; 2. consulting sports psychologists; 3. collecting open-ended responses

from samples of sports participants in several pilot studies. Fifty-eight items were collected from this process, then five graduate students of advanced sports psychology rated the items for content/clarity (and whether representative/appropriate for sport achievement motivation assessment) which resulted in 32 rated as definitely clear/appropriate by all raters. Responses were on a five-point scale, from 'strongly agree' to 'strongly disagree'; this was piloted, revised and the final version has 25 items.

▼ **Table 9.2** Dimensions measured with examples of items

Competitiveness	I am a competitive person
Goal orientation	I set goals for myself when I compete
Win orientation	Winning is important

University students: gained consent from class instructor, student participation voluntary. Second sample for test-retest comparisons to check reliability; 94% (205 of original 218) retook test. Some had changed classes or could not be contacted.

High school students: obtained from randomly selected classes and homerooms, purpose explained and asked for voluntary cooperation.

Ryan, R.M. and Deci, E.L. (2000) Self-determination theory, intrinsic motivation and well being

Background: Self-determination theory (SDT) views human nature as essentially positive, i.e. humans are inherently proactive and engaged (while acknowledging the converse, that people can also be passive and alienated). SDT stresses the importance of social-contextual conditions which can either facilitate or inhibit natural processes of self-motivation and healthy psychological development. SDT has used laboratory experiments and field studies (e.g. in teaching). Beyond our basic physiological needs, SDT identifies three essential psychological needs in the development of self-determination: competence, autonomy and relatedness. The extent to which these are present or absent affects the degree of self-determination/motivation.

1. Competence: (belief in) having a certain skill/ability (or, in the process of developing a skill).
2. Autonomy: (belief in) having some degree of choice/self-direction/control.
3. Relatedness: refers to some degree of security and support (e.g. an interested parent, caregiver, teacher) whereby encouragement is implicit.

(NB. Research findings confirm that satisfaction of needs is correlated with improved well-being.)

Self-determination, motivation, regulation of behaviour, locus of control and behaviour will **vary** with the activity/task, the social context, the social support and to some extent cognitive development, age, skill/ability level. So an individual might be highly self-determined and motivated on some occasions in some situations, but not necessarily in others.

SDT postulates two distinct types of motivation: 1) **intrinsic**: comes from within (internal)/not provided by others, usually arises spontaneously; 2) **extrinsic**: comes from outside the individual (external); can be positive (praise, rewards, payment, etc.) or negative (threats, coercion, criticism, etc.).

(NB. Research findings confirm that extrinsic motivators (e.g. money, tangible rewards) can diminish/damage intrinsic motivation e.g. Smith, Smoll & Curtis, 1979.)

Motivations need to be differentiated, e.g. in relation to a student's homework. An extrinsic motivator could be the student's chosen career, i.e. they choose to complete homework because they realise the value, compared to parental control (insisting on completion of homework).

Conclusion: Excessive control, lack of autonomy and lack of support (relatedness), and criticism will be inhibitory; opportunity for autonomy, positive feedback and support (relatedness) will enhance motivation and self-determination.

Evaluation: Theory based on extensive research (laboratory and field, wide variety of settings) with controls and standardisation, and can be considered reliable.

Debates: Nature (based on belief that interest, curiosity, activity is inherent), also nurture (what we learn/see modelled by others); situational explanations of behaviour. Less reductionist as it takes into account a variety of social factors as well as cognitive and developmental aspects of an individual. It is very useful for educators, sports psychologists, parents, health professionals and employers.

Results: Extensive statistical analysis completed to check reliability and validity, test-re-test correlations: a) competitiveness 0.89; b) win orientation 0.82; c) goal orientation 0.73 – i.e, a) and b) strong correlations, c) fairly strong – indicating reliability of measures. Measures consistently differentiated competitive and non-competitive participants and sports participants and non sports participants – indicating validity of measures.

Evaluation: Large sample sizes, mixed gender, inclusion of competitive and non-competitive, sports participants and non-sports participants and good age range means can generalise findings fairly widely. Researcher bias eliminated from extensive review process in devising measures.

Debates: Psychology as science – controls, standardisation, piloting, independent raters, test and re-test, extensive statistical analysis meet criteria (objectivity, falsifiability, replicability). Usefulness: useful for coaches to help assess athletes motivation. Less reductionist as it is multi-dimensional.

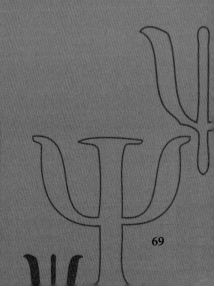

AROUSAL

Yerkes, R.M. and Dodson, J.D. (1908) The effects of electrically-stimulated arousal on learning in mice

Background: The 'fight or flight' response is considered as innate. Arousal is important to enhance performance, but it is well acknowledged that it can also inhibit performance.

Aim: To investigate the effects of shock levels on rapidity of learning, involving a discrimination task, in mice (and to establish the strength of shock which results in the fastest learning).

Sample/participants: 40 male and female mice aged 6–8 weeks (range 25–74 days).

Method/procedure: A series of laboratory experiments using an independent measures design. Four mice (two males, two females) in each condition. By using negative reinforcement (electric shock), mice were taught to discriminate between black and white doors of boxes. An electric shock (weak, medium or strong) was delivered if mice chose the black door. Each of 40 mice was given 10 tests every morning until it succeeded in choosing the white door/box correctly on three consecutive days (i.e. 30 tests).

Results: 1. The weak stimulus condition was discontinued after 20 days as only one of four mice had acquired habit (i.e. learned to choose white door/box). 2. Optimal learning (i.e. fewest number of trials required for habit formation – choosing white door/box) occurred with medium stimulation (arousal). 3. Slow habit formation (learning) resulted from both weak and strong stimulus conditions).

Evaluation: Series of experiments conducted to improve controls (e.g. varying levels of lighting) with much detailing of procedures could be replicated to check for reliability. Small numbers in each condition means reliability is questioned.

Issues: Ethics: could argue it is unethical to stress animals in research.

Debates: Nurture/situational explanation of behaviour. Not very useful as mice are distant from humans on the phylogenetic scale, although very useful concept that optimal amount of arousal will result in best performance.

Lacey, J.J. (1967) Somatic response patterning and stress

Lacey delivered this as a conference paper on psychological stress. He distinguishes different types of arousal.

▼ **Table 10.1** Types of arousal, measurements and behavioural indicators

Arousal type	How measured	Behavioural indicators
Electro-cortical	EEG (electroencephalogram) to record electrical activity in cortical area of brain	1. Confused thinking 2. Changes in attention or concentration
Autonomic	1. ECG (electroencephalogram) to measure heart rate or measure pulse 2. EMG (electromyogram) to measure muscle tension 3. GSR (galvanic skin response, to measure skin conductance) 4. Blood/urine analysis to identify changes in hormones/steroids, e.g. cortisol 5. Count respiration rate	1. Increased heart rate 2. Tension in muscles 3. Sweating (e.g. palms) 4. N/A 5. Increased breathing rate

The **3rd** type of arousal, **behavioural**, can be measured by **observation** and behavioural indicators are: deterioration in performance (e.g. accuracy, speed, co-ordination); restless pacing; fidgeting; nail biting; tremors (e.g. hands, legs); facial expressions (e.g. rigid 'smile', clenched teeth); changes in speech patterns (e.g. stuttering, hesitation); negative self-talk; biting/licking lips; rubbing palms on clothing; increased need to urinate.

Lacey stresses a number of important points (*NB. author's examples to illustrate*):

1. Arousal is not a unitary concept, i.e. can result in multiple somatic (bodily or physiological) responses (see table above).
2. Individual differences – there is great variation in individual arousal responses.
3. An individual might have variable arousal responses depending on changing context/social situation (e.g. performing in front of large audience/no audience) and/or outcomes (e.g. performance will determine team selection/financial reward/team promotion).
4. A measure of one type of arousal is not necessarily a valid measure of another.
5. Physiological changes are not necessarily arousal responses (e.g. increased breathing rate may be due to an athlete's rushing to performance area OR from 'warming-up' for performance; similarly, sweating).

Oxendine, J.B. (1980) Emotional arousal and motor performance

This paper presents summarised material from reviewed search and anecdotal evidence. One problem concerns definition as across this review researchers use different terms, e.g. motivation, excitement, arousal, drive. Oxendine uses emotional arousal (which you could argue has a cognitive/psychological component); however, essentially he is talking about conditions where 'normal' physiological functions are intensified and draws attention to both positive and negative effects.

Arousal and motor performance:

- Suggests that the optimum level of arousal will vary with, 1. the task and 2. the individual (e.g. high v. low trait anxiety, confidence; extrovert v. introvert).
- Cites Yerkes-Dodson law (which we now call 'Inverted-U'): complex tasks performed better when drive (arousal) is low, while simple tasks are performed better when drive (arousal) is high, and offers the following generalisation which extends this work:

  a) High level of arousal essential for optimal performance in gross motor activities involving strength, endurance and speed (e.g. weight-lifting, gymnast performing 'iron-cross').

  b) High level of arousal interferes with performances involving complex skills, fine muscle movements, coordination, steadiness and general concentration.

  c) Slightly above average level of arousal is preferable to normal or sub-normal arousal for all motor tasks.

Arousal effects on strength, endurance, speed:

- Cites story of mother lifting car off child, i.e. the notion that unusual feats of strength have been known in emergency situations, unrelated to expected performance of individual.
- Increased motivation improves performance.
- Fatigue results in performance deterioration; however, adrenaline can counteract effects, at least temporarily (e.g. Cannon's research, 1929, injecting adrenaline into fatigued animals).
- Confirms the difficulty of measuring arousal and speed; however, suggests that a frightened child is likely to run faster than one just told to run faster.
- Stress (over-arousal) is more detrimental when individuals are not acquainted with a task/activity, while experience in activity reduces adverse effects of stress.

Emotional arousal and performance in sports:

- Oxendine suggests that there is an optimal arousal level for some sports/skills, e.g. extreme arousal for rugby, sprinting and weight-lifting; slight arousal for golf, archery and shooting.

Evaluation: Suggestions arising out of research review might be considered as speculative and not necessarily reliable.

Debates: Individual explanations of behaviour. Acknowledging different types of arousal is less reductionist. Useful for coaches/managers to be able to identify behavioural signs of arousal/over-arousal in order to use intervention (e.g. relaxing breathing).

Exam tip

Although this sub-topic focuses on physiological arousal, you might acknowledge it is not possible to isolate this from psychological components of arousal as our cognitions/thoughts means we interpret situations (as stressful/not stressful). Link: Eysenck's biological basis for personality (arousal is level of activation in the autonomic nervous system).

ANXIETY

Martens, R. (1977) Sport Competition Anxiety Test (SCAT)

Background: Material here is summarised from a book, not a research paper.

Marten's aim was to develop an objective test of trait anxiety (A-trait) which minimises response bias and has clear scoring.

SCAT development: An early version was developed from use with 193 12–15-year-olds in junior high schools from Chicago, predominantly from white, middle class families. Items: (later version) questionnaire has 15 items (five of which are 'fillers') with possible response choices of 'rarely', 'sometimes', 'often' (# scored 1, 2 and 3; 'fillers' score 0).

▼ **Table 10.2** Examples of SCAT items

Trait-anxiety: 10 items (*reverse items)	Fillers, 'spurious' – five items (not measuring trait-anxiety, not scored)
2. Before I compete I feel uneasy 3. Before I compete I worry about not performing well 6. Before I compete I feel calm* 11. Before I compete I feel relaxed*	1. Competing against others is socially enjoyable. 13. Team sports are more exciting than individual sports

Scoring: Response scores are totalled (see above #) and would be designated either low level of anxiety, average level of anxiety or high level of anxiety. Reliability established via test and re-test, r=0.77. Eleven more studies are reported where SCAT construct validity was tested (i.e. confirmed testing what it intends to test – trait anxiety).

Evaluation: Test, re-test and construct validity tests extensive, therefore validity and reliability of SCAT well established. Scoring system is unambiguous and eliminates any interpretation bias. Reverse items to detect socially desirable responses/lying.
Debates: Individual explanations of behaviour. Reductionism – situations/social factors/state anxiety not taken into account. Can be considered useful (reliability and validity confirmed); however, less useful because only measuring trait anxiety; now subsumed in the up-dated CSAI-2.
Link: Personality.

Martens, R. *et al.* (1990) Competitive State Anxiety Inventory–2 (CSAI–2)

Background: SCAT is uni-dimensional (measures *trait* anxiety). Martens' original CSAI measured *state* anxiety. Other research confirmed the need for a multi-dimensional measure, as anxiety is *not* a unitary concept.

CSAI-2 is used to measure cognitive anxiety, somatic anxiety and self-confidence:

▼ **Table 10.3** CSAI-2

Measure	Example of item
Cognitive anxiety	'I am concerned about this competition', 'I am concerned about losing'
Somatic anxiety	'I feel at ease', 'I feel jittery', 'My body feels tense'
Self-confidence	'I'm confident I can meet the challenge', 'I feel self-confident'

Participants are instructed to respond how anxious they feel 'right now' and are given the response choices of:
1. 'Not at all', 2. 'Somewhat', 3. 'Moderately so', 4. 'Very much so'.
Researchers proposed that: 1. *Cognitive* anxiety has a negative linear relationship with performance (i.e. the higher the cognitive anxiety, the worse the performance). 2. *Somatic* anxiety has an inverted-U shaped relationship with performance (i.e. as somatic anxiety increases, so performance improves – up to an optimal point – after which continued increases in somatic anxiety lead to progressively worsening performance).
3. *Self-confidence* has a negative linear relationship with performance (i.e. the higher the self-confidence, the better the performance and vice versa).

To demonstrate that somatic and cognitive anxiety need to be *differentiated*, the CSAI-2 was used on athletes 48 hours, 24 hours, 2 hours and 5 minutes before an important competitive event.

Fazey, J. and Hardy, L. (1988) Catastrophe theory

Background: Many models of anxiety are based on, or have developed from the 'inverted-U' hypothesis (derived from Yerkes & Dodson, 1908). One difficulty in summarising/making comparisons is that researchers use different terms when investigating effects on performance of arousal or anxiety or stress, and it is not always clear whether distinctions are being made between the physiological and the psychological. Previous research would indicate the necessity of attending to: a) both cognitive and somatic aspects of anxiety; b) individual differences (e.g. self-esteem, confidence) and c) social context. According to the inverted-U hypothesis, where arousal or anxiety increases beyond the optimum point, performance *progressively* deteriorates. Catastrophe theory amends this and predicts that beyond the optimal point, further increases in arousal/anxiety result in a sudden, dramatic and catastrophic drop in performance. They introduce a new term 'hysteresis' – the process by which, following a dramatic collapse in performance, an athlete progressively re-builds performance back up.

(NB. Physiological arousal, when combined with high cognitive anxiety is most likely to lead to performance collapse. Cognitive anxiety is the key factor: it determines whether physiological effects are small (and manageable) or large (and catastrophic)).

An important addition to try and predict the effects of increased arousal/anxiety on performance is to take into account how well-learned the task is (Parfitt & Hardy, 1987). On **simple**, well-learned tasks the impact of physiological arousal is better managed and impacts less on performance. On **complex** or less well-learned tasks, the physiological arousal is more difficult to manage and performance is likely to be damaged.

Evaluation: Complex and difficult to test this theory empirically.
Debates: Individual explanations of behaviour (e.g. high/low confidence). More useful theory (than inverted-U) as in reality, performance rarely deteriorates little by little.

Exam tip

Other factors which are likely to interact and affect performance: age, general skill/ability level (differing effects on gross and fine motor skills, e.g. driving/putting in golf) novice/elite, evaluation apprehension, etc. Be prepared to distinguish trait and state anxiety: trait considered to be a personality characteristic and refers to the general level of anxiety experienced by an individual; state anxiety is that which is felt in response to specific stressful situations (which can be further divided into somatic state anxiety and cognitive state anxiety).

Results: These confirmed that cognitive anxiety remains fairly stable prior to the start; however, somatic anxiety started fairly low, but progressively increased.

Evaluation: This measure has been well used within sport and has been considered reliable; however, a revised version, CSAI-2R is considered more reliable. Statistical analysis of data eliminates researcher interpretation bias.
Debates: Less reductionist as the CSAI-2 does not just measure one concept. Useful for coaches/ trainers to be able to assess anxiety in order to use interventions (e.g. imagery, relaxation breathing) to reduce negative effects of anxiety on performance.

SELF-CONFIDENCE

Bandura, A. (1977) Self-efficacy theory

Background: Confidence has been considered a crucial factor to distinguish successful and unsuccessful athletes. Self-efficacy – the belief/expectation that you will be competent/successful in a particular task.

Theory: Bandura developed his theory from Behaviourism, believing that behaviour cannot be explained purely in terms of stimulus-response connections and reinforcement. Cognitions affect behaviour: individuals interpret/evaluate situations, particularly in terms of expected outcomes (positive outcomes, like winning, are likely to be worked towards; negative outcomes, like losing, may be avoided).

Four sources of self-efficacy expectations: 1. **Performance success:** If an athlete has been successful, they can believe they will be successful again. *Coach/sports psychologists can use statistics, medals, trophies, videos as reminders.* 2. **Vicarious experiences** (observing models): Seeing/understanding others (particularly those of similar skill/ability level) can achieve/perform allows an individual to believe that they will be able to perform also (especially when they are aware that another individual has had to overcome difficulties). *Kelly Holmes persisted through years of injury problems and won two gold medals in the 2004 Athens Olympic Games at the age of 34.* 3. **Verbal persuasion:** The influence of others encouraging an athlete ('you can do it!') is considered to be fairly weak; however, the belief of someone knowledgeable (e.g. coach, sports psychologist) can encourage an athlete to persevere. (*Andy Murray is known to 'self-talk' to encourage himself.*) 4. **Emotional arousal:** athletes will have greater belief/expectation in their ability to perform well when they can manage arousal/anxiety – this is crucial to improving self-efficacy.

These sources *combine* to increase expectations of success, which in turn affects performance. Self-efficacy is *dynamic* and varies with how these factors interact. An individual's expectations will determine how much effort they put in and also how long they are likely to persevere in the face of difficulties.

Evaluation: Considered useful – has been applied to sport and has been investigated by further research (Hepler & Chase, 2008).

Debates: theory is less reductionist as it considers a range of factors influential in self-efficacy. Free will (cognitions).

Links: Social Learning theory (SLT); personality factors, e.g. confidence, self-esteem, nACH.

▲ **Figure 10.1** Source of self-efficacy – performance success

Vealey, R.S. (1986) Sport confidence and competitive orientation

Background: Vealey developed an interactional sport-specific model of self-confidence which takes into account SC-trait (personality), competitive orientation (CO) and SC-state (confidence in particular situation).

Aim: To test model and to develop and validate a measure of sports confidence which accounts for individual differences.

Sample/participants: 666 (over five phases of testing; c. 200 in each of first four. Phase four participants same as phase two). Male and female; volunteers from a variety of sports (1. basketball, swimming, road racing; 2 and 4. basketball, tennis, softball, track/field; 3. members of PE classes and participants in competitive sport; 5. elite gymnasts). First four phase samples comprised high schools students, mean age c. 16–17 and college students, mean age c. 20.

Method/procedure: Phase 1: Inventory of items (using a five-point Likert scale) administered in a non-competitive situation, then c. 40 minutes prior to a competitive event. Phase 2: Used modified inventories (nine-point scale) and Social Desirability Scale in a non-competitive situation, then c. 40 minutes before competing. Phase 3: Purpose to test-retest for reliability (appropriate for trait and competitive orientation). Each sample divided into three groups, all tested than retested, one day later; one week later; one month later. Phase 4: In a non-competitive situation one group administered **trait** and CO inventories, SCAT and Physical Self-Efficacy Scale. Then, one hour prior to event, administered the **state** inventory and CSAI-2. Second group completed the **trait** and CO inventories a Self-esteem Scale and the Internal–External Control Scale in a non-competitive situation, followed by **state** inventory one hour prior to competition. Phase 5: Testing construct validity. Measures (**trait**, **state** and CO) completed 24 hours prior to competition; then 1.5 hours prior to first round of competition; then c. 2 hours after first round (and performance and satisfaction ratings, and causal attributions for performance). Objective performance scores from independent (competition) judges.

Woods, B. (2001) Imagery

Background: A variety of techniques are used by athletes, coaches and sports psychologists to help improve performance, one of which is imagery.

Woods outlines four functions of imagery:

1. Controlling arousal/anxiety: imagery is used alongside other techniques (e.g. relaxation breathing, progressive muscular relaxation (PMR), self-talk, cognitive re-labelling). It involves imagining/remembering particular circumstances of being/feeling relaxed, e.g. running along a beach on a training run or visualising their anxiety as an 'object' (e.g. a large balloon) which they envisage shrinking. This helps maintain focus on their performance and 'tune-out' distractions.

2. Mental practice: this involves cognitive rehearsal of skills/techniques, with no physical movement involved. Suspending time and motion, athletes can break down an action and mentally work through each sub-routine, imagining limb positions, correcting faults. More effective when athletes can involve other senses (kinaesthetic/bodily sensations, auditory and olfactory). Can re-run 'mistakes' with desirable outcome.

3. Understanding and retaining information: for many athletes, being able to create an image/picture in the mind helps reinforce learning.

4. Increasing self-confidence: imagery eliminates the stress of being watched/evaluated and any negative outcomes (e.g. making mistakes, losing); athlete feels prepared and confidence improved. Research suggests that combining imagery/mental practice with physical rehearsal is more effective than just physical practice on its own. Research has shown tiny muscle movements can be detected during mental practice of skill performance (Suinn, 1980). Useful when athlete is injured to keep techniques fresher in the mind.

Evaluation/debates: Useful – c. 90% of elite athletes use various imagery techniques to help control anxiety and improve their performance.
Link: Imagery can be seen as a conscious attentional narrowing (weapon focus).

Extend

Munroe-Chandler et al. (2008) investigated the relationship between imagery use and self-confidence and self-efficacy.

Results:
Phase 1: Confirmed measures were uni-dimensional constructs.
Phase 2: Trait and State measures – social desirability reduced to non-significant levels.
Phase 3: Trait reliability confirmed (mean co-efficient r=0.86); CO (performance) reliability confirmed (mean co-efficient r=0.69).
Phase 4: SC-trait effective predictor of SC-state. SC-trait positively related to perceived physical ability and confidence. Higher CO associated with internal locus of control, lower CO associated with external locus of control (significant negative correlation).
Phase 5: Significant correlations support SC-trait and CO as predictors of SC-state; high SC-trait athletes made more internal attributions (e.g. ability, effort) for performance than low SC-trait athletes.

Evaluation: Very useful – developed in a sporting context, with large samples (which are more reliable) across a range of sports, with varied ability. Limited age range, although appropriately targeted for performing athletes. Model allows for development/change.
Debates: Individual explanations of behaviour (confidence as trait). Psychology as science – extensive testing; re-testing for reliability and validity; statistical analysis; detailed procedures – meets criteria (reliability, falsifiability, replicability).

GROUP COHESION

Tuckman, B.W. (1965) Developmental sequences in small groups

Background: Tuckman was part of a think-tank of social psychologists studying small-group behaviour (for US Navy).

Aim: To review and evaluate literature on the developmental sequence in small groups and to extrapolate general concepts about group development.

Based on 50 available articles on groups – therapy (*c.* 26), training (*c.* 11) and natural and laboratory studies (*c.* 10). Tuckman produced summaries based on these three main categorisations, compared group summaries, then produced theory from commonalities across research. Many articles outlined four stages (some merged stages 3 and 4).

1. **Forming (orientation, testing and dependence)** – getting to know people, establishing new ties, being accepted (conforming), establishing group boundaries.

2. **Storming (intragroup conflict)** – characterised by argument, conflict; process of establishing 'pecking order'.

3. **Norming (development of group cohesion)** – co-operation starts to replace conflict; identification of common goals/ norms; consensual group action, mutual support.

4. **Performing (group work together)** – on task in hand; have established group identity that supports, rather than hinders, task.

5. *Adjourning (group termination)* – ceases to function, e.g. it disbands because of irreconcilable differences or because group task/goals have been achieved. This 5th stage was added in 1977 having reviewed additional research with co-author Jensen.

Evaluation: Unequal representation of types of groups. Most research involves single groups; data essentially qualitative rather than quantitative and lacks experimental rigour so cause and effect cannot be established. Time scales not comparable, e.g. laboratory studies conducted over a few hours, while some therapy groups lasted *c.* one year.
Debates: Availability of published articles were predominantly from western, industrialised, **individualistic** cultures, which means it would be ethnocentric to apply/generalise theory to **collectivist** cultures. Useful – applied in sport and other contexts. Theory derived from a large number of published studies and parallels (see link below) which confirms reliability to some extent.
Link: Forensic – Hastie's stages in (jury) decision-making.

Latane, B. *et al.* (1979) Social loafing

Background: A commonly held assumption is that individuals working collectively will produce greater effort than individuals working on their own, i.e. the presence of others will facilitate performance. Ringelmann's (1927) study investigated individual and group efforts on a rope pulling task and found the more individuals within a group, the less the individual effort.

▼ **Table 11.1** Ringelmann's results

No. of people	1	2	8
Total weight pulled	63 kg	117 kg	248 kg
Weight pulled per person	63 kg	59 kg	31 kg
Individual effort	100%	93%	49%

Aim: To investigate why collective effort is less productive than individual effort, i.e. social loafing.

Sample/participants: From Ohio State University. Experiment 1: 48 male undergraduates (studying introductory psychology). Experiment 2: 36 male undergraduate volunteers.

Method/procedure: *Experiment 1.* A conceptual replication of Ringelmann's work. Eight groups (tested separately) of six participants were seated in a large soundproofed laboratory and told to either clap or cheer as loudly as possible for five seconds. Practice allowed before completing 36 trials (each individual performed twice alone, four times in pairs, four times in 4's, six times in 6's), with the order of conditions counterbalanced. Measures taken by sound meter (in decibels, dB).

Experiment 2. In six groups of six participants were told study was investigating sensory feedback on production of sound in social groups; wore blindfolds and headsets (to prevent seeing/hearing); told room soundproofed and that other participants would not see/hear them; told to shout as loud as they could.

Carron, A.V. (1982) Cohesiveness in sports groups

Aim: To outline a conceptual perspective on cohesiveness and implications/limitations (constructs and future directions not covered here).

Definition: Cohesiveness is the tendency to stick together and remain united. Groups are social units and cohesiveness is the strength of the social bond within a group.

Need to acknowledge groups have (varying) goals/directives, i.e. some sort of common purpose. Cohesiveness is considered to be multi-dimensional. Festinger *et al.* (1963) argues two forces operate on a member to remain in a group: 1. attractiveness of group; and 2. the degree to which the group enables pursuit/attainment of a member's goals. So the two processes operating are 1. those associated with development of social relations, and 2. those associated with achievement of group objectives. Mikalachki (1969) distinguished these as *social* and *task* cohesion. This paper mentions a uni-dimensional measure – the Sports Cohesiveness Questionnaire (Martens *et al.,* 1972) where cohesiveness is a form of attractiveness (e.g. degree of friendship/attraction among group members). However, a better measure is the Group Environment Questionnaire (GEQ, Carron *et al.,* 1985) which is multi-dimensional, measuring four aspects of cohesion, including social and task cohesion.

Carron's model seeks to accommodate a wide range of factors likely to impact on group cohesion.

1. Environmental factors (e.g. contracts, organisational 'culture') – these affect **2. Personal factors** (e.g. individual differences, need for satisfaction) and **3. Leadership factors** (e.g. leadership style and behaviour relationships, both 'coach-athlete' and 'coach-team'). All of these are likely to affect **4. Team factors** (e.g. team stability and ability, group task, desire for group success and group orientation) which will impact **5. Cohesion** (both task and social) and **6. Group outcomes** (e.g. team stability, effectiveness of team performance and relative performance effectiveness) and **7. Individual outcomes** (satisfaction, effectiveness of performance, relative performance effectiveness and behavioural consequences).

This model allows for on-going change, e.g. group outcomes (winning or losing) are likely to impact on future team factors, group (social) cohesion, personal factors and individual outcomes – imagine feedback loops.

Debates (and evaluation): Model (and GEQ) less reductionist and more useful. Social determinism/situational explanations of behaviour.
Link: Tuckman – social cohesion activities early in group formation process; task cohesion in later stages.

Extend
Carron et al. (2002) study on team cohesion and team success.

Discussion: Zajonc's social facilitation theory (suggesting that people are aroused by the presence of others and are likely to work harder) is not upheld. These results could be explained either by social loafing or by confounding variables of lack of coordination/efficiency (as could Ringelmann's) or social conformity.
Evaluation: Controls, standardisation and replication means results can be considered reliable. Fairly small sample sizes means cannot generalise findings. Laboratory study lacks ecological validity which means cannot generalise.
Debates: Social determinism/situational explanations of behaviour. Ethnocentric – may not be applicable to collectivist cultures.

Results: *Experiment 1:* Statistical analysis (of variance) revealed that as group size increased, so sound generated per person decreased (significant at 0.1% level).

▼ **Table 11.2** Noise produced in relation to group size

Group size	Mean noise level (dB)	% of individual capacity
1	3.7	(100)
2	2.6	71
4	1.8	51
6	1.5	40

Experiment 2: Reported as similar to *Experiment 1.*

AUDIENCE EFFECTS

Cottrell, N.B. *et al.* (1968) Social facilitation of an audience

Background: Experiments have shown that the presence of an audience affects performance by increasing an individual's drive.

Aim: To evaluate Zajonc's proposal (earlier research) that mere presence is sufficient to affect performance.

Sample/participants: 45 male, introductory psychology students at Kent State University, USA, participating to fulfil a course requirement.

Method/procedure: Laboratory experiment using an independent measures design. Participants assigned randomly to three conditions (15 in each): 'alone', 'audience' and 'mere presence'; told study is about how people learn a foreign language. Nonsense words (e.g. LOKANTA, ZABULON) were presented as a) training stimuli, on 4" x 6" photos of each word; then participants were tested on words; b) test stimuli were 2" x 2" slides of each word. Word presented by photo, read aloud by experimenter; participants had to read aloud. Rate of 1 every 4 seconds. presented tachistoscopically. 'Alone' condition: participant alone during testing. 'Audience' condition: two confederates in experimental room (posing as participants waiting for colour-perception experiment; told not to talk). 'Mere presence' condition: two confederates in experimental room who wore blindfolds (also posing as participants and told not to talk). 120 responses for each participant. Data analysed statistically.

Results: 'Audience' condition performance better than 'mere presence'/'alone' (little to distinguish these conditions, i.e. not significant). Presence of audience enhanced performance on every trial block, while performance for 'mere presence' and 'alone' conditions was similar.

Conclusion: Zajonc's proposal about mere presence being sufficient to enhance drive (and performance) is **not** upheld. Other factors must be involved, e.g. an audience that is interested/watching/evaluating. Further research is required.

Evaluation: Small number in each condition not reliable, gender biased and geographically specific. Laboratory experiment lacks ecological validity. High level of control and standardisation means can have more confidence in results.

Debates: Social determinism/situational explanations of behaviour (presence/absence of others). Reductionism – (ignores individual differences, e.g. self-confidence). Useful to clarify Zajonc's proposal.

Zajonc, R.B. *et al.* (1969) Social enhancement impairment of performance in the cockroach

Background: In an earlier (1965) social facilitation paper, Zajonc reviews research on audience and co-action effects and avoidance learning.

Aim: To test the drive theory of social facilitation, i.e. increased drive (arousal) will enhance performance. *(NB. Only one of two experiments reported is summarised here.)*

Sample/participants: 72 adult female cockroaches.

Method/procedure: Laboratory experiment using an independent measures design. IVs: 'co-action' or 'audience' condition; straight runway or maze. Baseline established by timing each cockroach over 10 'alone' trials on straight runway (mean used). Control group of 20 cockroaches (not exposed to passive audience) timed with audience boxes in position, run individually.

▼ Table 11.3 Sample distribution across conditions

N = 72	Co-acting (32)	Audience (40)
Runway	16	20
Maze	16	20

Roaches placed at start end of runway (lit from behind), opposite end was dark goal box (which cockroaches would aim for as they are photophobic, i.e. repelled by light).

'Co-action' condition: two cockroaches placed simultaneously at end of runway and timed (mean of 10 trials used). 'Audience' condition: with cockroach grandstand at the side of runway (each cockroach in separate compartments; air holes to allow olfactory cues; mean of 10 trials used). 'Maze' (two straight runways, intersecting at 90 degrees, with goal box situated at end of intersecting runway).

Schwartz, B. and Barsky, S.F. (1977) The home advantage

Background: The 'home advantage' concept was recognised but had not been systematically investigated.

Aim: To investigate the home advantage in organised sports.

Sample: From 1971, 1880 baseball games, 182 professional football games, 910 college football games; from 1971–72, 542 hockey games; from 1952–66, 1485 basketball games.

Method/procedure: Indirect observation, i.e. data collected for another purpose.

▼ **Table 11.5** Percentage of games won/lost/tied by home team in three sports (number of games in brackets)

	Sport			
	Baseball	**Football (Professional)**	**Football (College)**	**Hockey**
Home team outcome	1971	1971	1971	1971–72
Win	53% (989)	55% (100)	59% (532)	53% (286)
Lose	47% (891)	41% (74)	40% (367)	30% (163)
Tie		4% (8)	1% (11)	17% (93)
Total no. of games	**(1880)**	**(182)**	**(910)**	**(542)**

Source: Schwartz and Barsky (1977) 'The Home Advantage', *Social Forces* 55(3). Reproduced with permission of Oxford University Press.

Results: If there was no 'home advantage'/no disadvantage to playing away, you would expect wins/losses to be c. 50%. The home advantage differs from sport to sport –the smallest advantage was observed in baseball and the biggest advantage in hockey. Additional win/loss data from four sports was obtained and further analysis was conducted (because time limited data, i.e. 1971–72); this confirmed a higher percentage of home wins and a 'home advantage'. Basketball data, based on the performance of the 'Big Five' teams, are categorised differently as games are played at: i) home, ii) 'neutral' ground and iii) away. However, the home advantage is confirmed with an 82% win rate (based on 354 games). Sources of home advantage are considered, e.g. i) familiarity with ground/arena, ii) travel fatigue for away team (both discounted – i) basketball/hockey arenas very similar; ii) comparisons of first and second half of season reveal little difference), while iii) moral support from spectators was confirmed as main factor (based on analysis of audience size and relationship to performance).

Evaluation: Objective data, not liable to researcher/interpretation bias. Not generalisable across all sports and cannot apply findings to individual sports.
Debates: Social determinism/situational explanations of behaviour (playing home or away). Useful – for coaches to work on the 'away' disadvantage.

Results: Statistical analysis (of variance). Results consistent with drive theory of social facilitation, i.e. presence of others enhances performance with dominant response/well learned (or easy task – runway); presence of others inhibits performance when task not well learned (hard task – maze). Performance (running time) better in co-acting (than audience condition).

▼ **Table 11.4** Cockroaches (mean) running time in seconds

	Task			
	Runway		Maze	
	Alone	**Social**	**Alone**	**Social**
Co-acting	40.58	32.96	110.45	129.46
Audience	62.65	39.30	221.35	296.64

Source: Zajonc *et al.* (1969) adapted.

Evaluation: Controls and standardisation would allow replication to check reliability. Cockroaches not close to humans on phylogenetic scale, therefore not generalisable (and not very useful).
Debates: Social determinism/situational explanation of behaviour (presence of others; conditions). Useful – having established theory, provides basis for research with humans.

Stogdill, R.M. (1948) Personal factors associated with leadership

Background: A key question is whether leaders are born (nature) or made (nurture). The 'Great Man' theory considers leaders are born.

Aim: To identify traits and characteristics of leadership.

Method: A survey/review of literature.

Sample (literature): The bibliography cites 124 references (studies only included where factors were studied by three or more investigators).

The number of studies and 'age' of participants (where information is specified) was: 3 pre-school, 17 elementary school, 34 high school, 26 college students and 32 adults. The references cover a wide time span (summarised here by number and decade of publication): 2, 1900–9; 3, 1910–19; 30, 1920–9; 57, 1930–9; 32, 1940–7.

Research: Published in recognised journals of psychology, sociology, teaching/education and business (and some books, e.g. Cattell's (1946) *Description and measurement of Personality*).

Types of leaders: Research covers political/community leaders, businessmen, army officers, farmers and gangs – most adult studies involve white, Caucasian males. *(NB. School/student research generally involved male and female; a few involved female samples only; two or three studies on North American Indians and African Americans.)*

Geographical spread: the majority involved participants in USA (some British; handful of European).

The author has categorised the 'methods/procedures' used as 1) Observation in situations which allow leaders to emerge; 2) Choice – voting/ naming preferred leader (by group members); 3) Nomination/rating by qualified observers (i.e. those in formal position to identify leader); 4) Selection (or rating/testing) of individuals in leadership positions; 5) Analysis of biographical and case history data; 6) Listing of traits/characteristics considered essential to leadership. In addition, interviews, questionnaires, psychometric measures (intelligence/personality tests) and statistical analysis used, including correlation.

Results: From 29 factors, there is contradictory evidence. However, a brief summary of the commonalities among 'leaders' concludes they are:
1. More intelligent than other members (but not too much more); 2. Generally have better grades; 3. More dependable; 4. More sociable/participate better in group; 5. Have better practical knowledge (relative to leader situation); 6. More confident; 7. More persistent.
(NB. Interestingly, the qualities, characteristics and skills required are determined, to a great extent, by the demands of the leadership situation.)

Evaluation: Large 'sample', broad based (subject and context); however not gender balanced over age range, and culturally restricted (individualistic-type cultures). Out-of-date and therefore less useful.
Debates: Individual explanations of behaviour (personality characteristics/traits) and situational. Reductionist – does not investigate situation/social context. It would be ethnocentric to generalise/apply findings as research. Commonalities due to nurture?

Results: 1. **Observed CBAS behaviour** differences – trained coaches (positively) reinforced significantly more than controls (5% level). 2. **Players' perceptions** (coaching behaviours) – trained coaches were rated as engaging more frequently in 'Reinforcement' and 'General technical instruction' than controls and less frequently in 'Punishment' and 'Punitive technical instruction' (differences consistent with training programme guidelines). 3. **Players' attitudes:** Trained-coach children reported greater enjoyment in playing and a stronger desire to play next season; also rated their coaches as better teachers. 4. **Players' self-esteem:** no significant differences in (end-season) self-esteem; however, changes in selfiesteem (involving test, re-test over 12 months) found significant increases with trained-coach children (1% level). 5. **Win/loss data** comparisons made (to eliminate as possible confounding variable) and *no* statistically significant difference found between groups.

Smith, R.E. *et al.* (1979) Coach-effectiveness training: a cognitive-behavioural approach

Background: With the development of organised sport for youngsters, the quality of coaching is crucial to beneficial outcomes.

Aim: To develop and assess an experimental training programme to enhance coach effectiveness.

Sample/participants: 34 males coaching 'Little League' (10–12 and 13–15-year-olds) baseball; from Seattle area; mean age *c.* 36; average of *c.* 8 years' coaching experience. Three left during study (due to team mergers/moving house) from control group. 325 players interviewed (82%).

Method/procedure: Field experiment using an independent measures design (and observation and self-reports: questionnaires and interviews). Coach training programme empirically derived from a previous investigation (Smith *et al.*, 1978). Coaches: recruited by invitation and randomly assigned: 18 to experimental/trained group, 16 to control/not trained group. Trained (pre-season) for two hours (by researchers): programme stressed reinforcement (positive), encouragement and technical instruction (and to reduce fear of failure).

Coaches observed during first two weeks' of season (used CBAS – Coaching Behaviour Assessment System, Smith *et al.,* 1977) and feedback was given. Coaches also completed self-monitoring forms.

Observers: 16 undergraduates trained to observe coaches over four weeks in CBAS training material and behavioural scoring. 26,412 behaviours were coded from four games (per coach).

Players' perceptions/attitudes: assessed in structured, end-season interviews with trained interviewers ('blind' to experimental conditions). Rating scales on recall of coaching behaviour and self-esteem. Extensive statistical analysis.

Evaluation: High levels of control, statistical analysis means we can have greater confidence in results, however, small sample of coaches (all male, geographically specific), only baseball means need to be careful in applying/generalising findings (and less useful). **Debates:** Social determinism/situational explanations of behaviour (coaches' behaviour). Useful as basis for replication/future research.

Chelladurai, P. (1978) A multi-dimensional model of leadership

Background: The trait approach has been discounted as insufficient to explain leadership. An early study by Lewin *et al.* (1939) was useful in identifying the effects of different *styles* of leadership on group performance.

Autocratic style (authoritarian, controlling) resulted in most productive groups, however productivity declined when leader absent. **Democratic** style (members consulted/involved, feel they have some say) resulted in a less productive group, but productivity continued in absence of leader. **Laissez-faire** style ('anything goes', i.e. **no** leadership) resulted in the least productive group and with the most conflict within the group.

Later research identified person-oriented and task-oriented leaders (Fiedler, 1967), setting the scene for 'contingencies', i.e. leadership is dependent (contingent) upon a range of factors, e.g. nature of the task, group needs, style of leader, situation/context.

Aim: To provide a multi-dimensional model of leadership, identifying contingent factors and how they interact in a sporting context.

Model outlines *possible* leader behaviours: **Prescribed:** where leader conforms to the expectations/rules of the organisation (e.g. sport governing body). **Preferred:** leader behaviour led/driven (at least partially) by group members' preferences (although situation would have some impact also). **Actual:** behaviour engaged in by leader (considered to be driven by traits/innate characteristics).

Chelladurai introduces the notion of *congruence* to explain how these possible behaviours might 'fit' together.

Model suggests four leadership scenarios and the likely outcomes:

1. When prescribed, actual and preferred behaviour are **congruent** then 'everyone's happy' and performance is likely to be good.

2. When prescribed, actual and preferred behaviour are **incongruent** then 'no-one's happy', the team/ governing body will be dissatisfied, the leader will not be effective, the team performance will be poor and the leader is likely to be dismissed.

3. When leadership behaviour is incongruent with prescribed, but congruent with actual and preferred then the team is satisfied initially, however, governing body dissatisfaction means the leader's authority will be in question, the team will lose confidence and over time performance may deteriorate.

4. When prescribed and preferred leadership behaviour is congruent, but actual is incongruent then group members and the governing body will be dissatisfied, performance will be poor, and the leader may be removed.

The model also acknowledges the leaders' characteristics and the influence of context/situation.

Evaluation: Less reductionist (many factors) therefore more useful.
Debates: Situational/individual explanation of behaviour (context and leader traits taken into account).

EXERCISE AND PATHOLOGY

Bernstein, L. (1994) Physical exercise and reduced risk of breast cancer

Background: Physical activity effects the production of sex hormones. Exercise/training: reduces length of phases of hormone production; lowers hormone levels; can reduce frequency of ovulation; can delay onset of menstruation – reducing cumulative exposure to progesterone and oestradiol, thought to be associated with breast cancer risk.

Aim: To determine whether women regularly participating in physical exercise during reproductive years had a reduced risk of breast cancer (compared to inactive women).

Sample/participants: 545 women (aged 40 or under at diagnosis), newly diagnosed with breast cancer; Los Angeles area (targeted those born USA, Canada or Europe/white); 545 controls

(matched on date of birth within 36 months; race; whether had children/or not; neighbourhood of residence).

Method/procedure: Experiment using an independent measures design (matched pairs). Doctors' permission given to contact patients via letter; follow-up phone call. Interviews competed with 744 breast cancer patients (78.4% of living eligible patients) – participants only included where *complete* histories on physical exercise obtained. 11.5% refused to take part (111). Interviews, conducted by same female nurse-interviewer (consent obtained/research approved), took history of exercise participation; medical case histories (reproductive and contraceptive information) obtained. Mean number of hours per week exercise calculated for each participant (from start of menstruation to one year prior to breast cancer diagnosis).

Results: The mean age at which women were diagnosed was 36.0 years for both experimental and control groups: 63% diagnosed 36–40 years old; c. 29% diagnosed 31–35. Potentially confounding variables investigated during statistical analysis (age at first menstruation; age at first-term pregnancy; number of full-term pregnancies; months of lactation; family history of breast cancer: mother/sister or adopted). No evidence found linking age of first menstruation, contraceptive use or child-bearing with risk of breast cancer.

Evaluation: Question validity of self-reports (and problems with memory/recall). Sample geographically specific (and white) so cannot generalise.
Debates: Useful to have risk information to educate. Less reductionist: investigates a range of factors (child- bearing, contraception); however, still somewhat reductionist as it does not investigate other factors (diet, alcohol/drug consumption). Biological determinism (hormones) and social determinism (factors 'inducing' exercise participation), also nature and nurture.

▼ Table 12.1

Hours of exercise per week	Reduces risk of pre-menopausal breast cancer by
1–3 hours	c. 30%
4 hours	› 50%

(NB. Relative to inactive women)

Results: 1. Aerobic and weight-training groups: physical self-efficacy*, mood*, life satisfaction* *significantly* higher than Controls; 2. comparisons of pre- and post- programme measures (physical self-efficacy, positive mood, life satisfaction) increased. Aerobic group reported higher life satisfaction than weight-training group. 3. Controls: Stretch/flex group: self-reports revealed decline on all three* measures.

Lox, C.L. *et al.* (1995) Exercise and psychological well-being in HIV patients

Background: Negative mood-states (e.g. depression) can inhibit optimal immune-system functioning. As HIV is an immune-system infection, regular exercise is considered to both stimulate its functioning as well as having positive effects on mood states.

Aim: To improve mood states/well-being of HIV patients by implementing (different) 12-week exercise programmes (action research).

Sample/participants: 33 patients diagnosed with HIV.

Method/procedure: Experiment using an independent measures design (with self-report/questionnaire measures). Participants randomly

Hausenblas, H.A. and Carron, A.V. (1999) Eating disorders in athletes

Background: Previous research on eating disorders comparing athletes and non-athletes has been inconclusive.

Aim: To conduct a meta-analysis (review) of literature on eating disorders (bulimia, anorexia, 'drive for thinness') in male and female athletes.

Sample (literature): 92 studies (based on 10,878 athletes; mixed/single gender; use of control groups; fifty-eight different sports/activities; varied sample sizes, 11–745; competing levels from high school/club to regional/elite).

Key questions:
Are athletes at higher risk than non-athletes of developing eating disorders? Some psychological characteristics/personality traits are considered advantageous for athletic performance (perfectionism, compulsiveness, self-motivation, high need to achieve). These same characteristics are associated with individuals with eating disorders (Leung *et al.*, 1996). In addition, a consequence of high activity is a (temporary) suppression of appetite.

Are certain groups of athletes at more risk of developing eating disorders? Consider sports a) with weight classifications (rowing, boxing); b) where weight/body size is important to performance success (distance running, cycling, jockeys); c) with aesthetic 'ideals' (gymnasts, figure skaters).

Method/procedure: Literature search conducted in relevant databases. Meta-analysis using extensive statistical testing. A correction factor was calculated (ES – effect size) so that the effects found in small samples (which are positively biased) did not statistically overestimate the true effect when comparisons made between research. Studies used three measures of eating disorder: anorexia, bulimia (DSM-IV definitions) and 'drive for thinness' (Garner & Rosen, 1991). Sports classified into six categories based on sport-specific demands: aesthetic, endurance, ball game, weight-dependent, power and technical.

Results:
1. Female athletes reported more bulimic and more anorexic symptomatology than non-athlete controls (no differences found between competition levels).
2. Female athletes and non-athletes did not differ on 'drive for thinness'.
3. Male athletes reported more bulimic symptomatology than non-athlete controls (no differences found between competition levels) and a small effect was found for report of anorexic symptomatology.
4. More male athletes reported 'drive for thinness' than non-athlete controls.
5. Males in 'aesthetic', 'endurance' and 'weight-dependent' sports had significantly higher 'drive for thinness' than non-athletic controls (5% level).

Evaluation: Control for ES and extensive statistical analysis means can consider study more reliable. Useful covering extensive range of sports/activities, males and females and different competition levels.
Debates: Nurture (learn cultural ideas about ideal body shapes/sizes). Social determinism/ situational explanations of behaviour (ideals 'drive' eating).
Link: Personality (some traits associated with successful athlete are common to individuals with eating disorders).

Extend
Sundgot-Borgon and Klungland Torstveit (2004) eating disorders in Norwegian elite athletes.

allocated to groups: 1. aerobic exercise; 2. weight-training; 3. stretch/flexibility (**control**).

Measures taken: 1. Physical self-efficacy, six-point Likert scale (Ryckman *et al.*, 1982); 2. and 3. Questionnaires on mood states and life satisfaction (all three measures taken before and after the programme) and 4. additional questionnaire (e.g. how long HIV diagnosis known, current relationship(s), involvement in counselling/support).

Participants instructed to complete exercise regime three times per week for 45 minutes and to record details on a worksheet. Controls (stretch/flex) were instructed *not* to engage in any other form of exercise.

Evaluation: Small numbers in each group, question reliability. Good use of control group to establish baseline. Self-reports means validity can be questioned.
Debates: Social determinism/situational explanations of behaviour.
Link: self-efficacy (Bandura).

EXERCISE AND MENTAL HEALTH

Steinberg, H. and Sykes, E. (1985) The endorphin hypothesis

Background: Endorphin research has been multi-disciplinary, highly complex and characterised by a lack of consensus.

Aim: This is a report on the first symposium on 'Endorphins and behaviour', (comprising five papers/research presented by authors currently working in the field) held by the British Psychological Society in 1985. It also reviews literature and its main focus is endorphins and exercise.

The **physiological** response to exercise is the production of beta-endorphin (a natural 'painkilling' substance) which can be interpreted **cognitively** as a 'high'/feeling good.

The endorphin hypothesis states that sustained/vigorous exercise can i) produce an emotional 'high' (feeling of euphoria/enthusiasm); ii) can result in increased tolerance to pain; iii) may become 'addictive'.

Mood: Research has established that exercise can induce positive moods in normal subjects and have anti-depressant effects in depressed patients. The notion of 'runners' high' (popularly accepted), despite vast documentation, has not yet had validity conclusively established.

Analgesia: Pain perception decreases during periods of stress confirmed by, for example, a study on long-distance runners (Janal *et al.,* 1984).

Addiction: The evidence has not been either systematic or conclusive because of problems involving participant's motivations, expectations, etc. There is the suggestion that the psychological profile/personality of addicts (whether narcotics or exercise) may be similar (Pargman & Baker, 1980).

Method/procedure: Typical measurements have included self-reports (questionnaires/interviews, using a variety of scales, mainly quantitative data) and analysis of blood plasma.

Results: Measurements from blood samples, pre- and post-exercise, showed increases in beta-endorphin levels (as well as hormones ACTH, prolactin and growth hormone). There are individual differences in beta-endorphin increases in response to exercise and measurements have varied considerably depending on exact post-exercise time of blood sample collection.

Evaluation: Difficulties in comparing research with different methodologies. Validity of self-report measurements in question. Alternative explanations challenge hypothesis, e.g. BDNF may be linked to mood; exercise can improve self-esteem.
Debates: Useful (exercise programmes recommended as part of treatment for depression). Biological determinism (hormones) and social determinism (factors 'inducing' exercise participation, beliefs); also nature and nurture.
Link: personality.

Leith, L.M. and Taylor, A.H. (1990) Review of the psychological aspects of exercise

Background: The endorphin hypothesis suggests the benefits in well-being, derived from exercise, are limited by the extent to which exercise is sustained and vigorous.

Aim: To review research studies (from previous decade) into the effects of exercise on mental health; to identify and evaluate consistent findings.

Sample (literature): 81 research studies identified from internet search on appropriate databases; based on a wide range of participants (e.g. male/female, children/teenagers/adults, students, psychiatric patients, alcoholics) using varying sample sizes.

Method/procedure: Research was categorised into: pre-experimental, quasi-experimental and experimental for comparison/evaluation purposes. A wide range of measures was used across research, some of which are: Beck's Depression Inventory (Beck *et al.,* 1961), Cattell's 16PF (Cattell, 1956), Profile of Mood States (POMS, Morgan, 1979), State-Trait Anxiety Inventory (Spielberger *et al.,* 1971).

Results:

1. Pre-experimental: in 7 out of 9 studies, a significant improvement in mental health measures was found (i.e. reduced anxiety and depression).
2. Experimental: 13 out of 26 studies found significant improvements in well-being (e.g. self-concept in children).
3. Quasi-experimental: of 46 studies (using mostly student samples), over 75% showed improvements in mood states and self-concept.

Morgan, W.P. (1979) Mental health model

Background: Research was becoming more interested in the predictive power of psychological testing.

Aim: To test the mental health model and investigate whether successful athletes would score *high* on vigour and extroversion, *low* on anger, anxiety, conformity, confusion, depression, tension and neuroticism.

Sample/participants: 57 rowers attending the elite national training camp.

Method/procedure: 57 out of 60 volunteered and completed the Minnesota Multiphasic Personality Inventory (MMPI), having been told their results would not be used/available as part of the team selection. Team selections were made *before* profiles analysed.

Results: 10 out of 16 successful and 31 out of 41 unsuccessful athletes were identified by these measures, i.e. successful athletes' profile followed the prediction and scored high on vigour and extroversion, while unsuccessful athletes' profiles were the opposite (i.e. generally scored lower on vigour and extroversion, higher on anger, anxiety, conformity, confusion, depression, tension and neuroticism).

Evaluation: Lack of control group in two-thirds of pre-experimental (could not establish cause and effect); lack of random allocation to groups (e.g. quasi-experimental category). Most studies reductionist as other measures (e.g. exercise type, improvements in fitness, exercise duration) not investigated.
Debates: Social determinism/situational explanations of behaviour.
Link: self-efficacy (Bandura).

Conclusion: MMPI can be used to predict successful and unsuccessful athletes.
Evaluation: Self-report measures have validity problems (although the control of MMPI not being used prior to selection helps). The mental health model has proved useful in predicting successful/ unsuccessful athletes.
Additional research: 1. conducted on US prospective candidates for Olympic wrestling team (Nagle, 1975). Wrestlers completed the POMS (Profile of Mood States) and successful athletes scored higher on positive mood (i.e. vigour) and lower on negative moods (i.e. anger, confusion, depression, fatigue and tension) than non-successful. In 1976, wrestlers again completed this measure, with similar profile results.
2. Long-distance runners (Morgan & Pollock, 1977) completed the POMS and the profile of successful runners was similar.
The 'iceberg' profile – the name given to the profile of successful athletes.

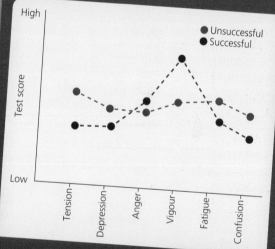

▲ **Figure 12.1** Profile of Mood States (POMS) scores, illustrating successful and unsuccessful athletes

Debates: It would be ethnocentric to apply/generalise the findings from individualistic-culture research – successful athletes from collectivist cultures may not have the same/similar profile. These self report measures (POMS, MMPI) are reductionist – they do not take account of serious life events which might be responsible for some measures (e.g. depression resulting from death/loss).
Link: Personality.

Extend/exam tip

Boeker et al.'s (2008) research using PET scans or long-distance runners (confirming endorphins as being implicated with mood change). Improved psychological health may, in part, be due to increase in self-efficacy, social interaction with others, distraction (from worries) and increased production of neurotransmitters (e.g. serotonin and dopamine).

ISSUES IN EXERCISE AND SPORT

Costill, D.L. *et al.* (1991) The influence of training volume on swimming performance

Background: Coaches and athletes generally assume that training more frequently, and with more intensity, will result in improved performance.

Aim: To investigate the effects of training volume.

Sample/participants: 24 male collegiate swimmers, Ball State University, USA.

Method/procedure: Field Experiment (matched pairs design). Participants matched (on stroke speciality, skill, prior training experience) then divided into two groups: *Long* and *Short*. First four weeks' of training, groups trained together (once daily, *c*. 1.5 hours); next six weeks the *Short group* continued with the same schedule, while the *Long group* trained twice daily (1.5 hours a.m., 1.5 hours p.m.). Swimmers tested on wide range of measures over whole programme: swimming power (measured during tethered swimming by Cybex machine); heart rate; blood pressure; muscle biopsies; blood samples; competition performance (which was part of normal schedule) was compared with previous seasons' best performances. Pre-training and base-line measures were taken.

Results: Statistical analysis of variance used. Major finding: additional training completed by **Long group** did not produce a greater improvement in performance compared to *Short group*.

▼ **Table 12.2** Condensed summary of results on Short versus Long training volume (significance level 5%)

Test	Short	Long
Competitive Performance	Significant improvement over previous season	Significant improvement over previous season
Swimming power (mean, weeks 1–25)	18.4% improvement (and significantly *higher* than long)	11.6% improvement (and significantly *lower* than short)
Cortisol (stress)	Levels remained stable	Significant *increase*
Maximal sprint velocity	Mean improvement 3.9%	Mean improvement 3.7%
Distance per stroke	16.6% (significant difference)	15.7% (significant difference)

Long group experienced a decline in sprinting performance during increased training weeks 5–11.

Evaluation: Cannot generalise findings to females, under 16s, other sports/countries; small sample not reliable. Objective physiological testing and performance measures not liable to researcher/interpretation bias, therefore more reliable.

Debates: Useful – suggesting there is an optimal amount of training which may vary with event distance and dangers of increased stress from higher training loads (possible 'burnout').

Hart, E.A. *et al.* (1989) Measuring social physique anxiety

Background: Dissatisfaction with physique might encourage individuals to participate in exercise. However, physique anxiety might impede them, (while confidence might enhance participation).

Aim: To assess physique anxiety when being observed or evaluated (and to develop and evaluate a Social Physique Anxiety Scale – SPAS).

Sample/participants: Undergraduates, USA. Study 1: Pilot/scale development (22-items) 195 (97 females, 98 males). Revised 12-item scale, 89 (46 females, 43 males) and replication (56 male/female). Study 2: 93 males, 94 females. Study 3: 56 women (28 high score, 28 low score on SPAS), mean age 18.4 years.

Method/procedure: Study 1: Scale development. 30 items evaluated by knowledgeable individuals on clarity, content validity, gender appropriateness; 22 items were piloted. Statistical analysis confirmed

Results: Study 1: Statistical analysis confirmed reliability. Study 2: Statistical analysis confirmed construct validity (and validity). Study 3: Significant differences: High scoring SPAS women reported being more stressed during physique evaluation (than low scoring SPAS women); also felt less comfortable during evaluation; reported more negative thoughts about their body's appearance.

High scoring SPAS women's anxieties partly justified (based on significantly higher weight and higher body fat percentage than low-scoring SPAS women).

Maganaris, C.N. *et al.* (2000) Expectancy effect and strength training

Background: Huge pressures on elite athletes to improve their performance may encourage the illegal use of anabolic steroids.

Aim: To investigate expectancy effects on performance.

Sample/participants: 11 male, UK National level, power lifters (in regular training) aged 19–23, (trained together for two years prior to investigation; confirmed never having used illegal performance aids).

Method/procedure: Investigation instigated by athletes approaching (well-trusted) coach asking about the use of anabolic steroids (AS). Full clearance sought (ethics committees) and given, because participants were considering AS use and the investigation had potential to dissuade athletes from using performance-enhancing drugs. Athletes told there would be no harmful effects. Fourteen days prior to start, participants instructed to discontinue use of dietary supplements; training diaries inspected and dietary record sheets assessed for nutritional intake (control measures of possible confounding variables).

Trial 1: Participants given two saccharin tablets, five minutes prior to test lifting; told it was a powerful, quick-acting AS; then completed lifts (bench press, dead lift, squat) under competition conditions, in presence of coach. Given two more tablets after and told they were 'for use during subsequent week's training'. Average daily energy intake was monitored.

Trial 2: Seven days' later, participants interviewed about training. Then split into two groups: AS/AS and AS/P. This time the second group were told the tablets were saccharin/a placebo.

(NB. Participants fully debriefed at end of study; told performance improvements due to improved confidence, not pharmaceutical 'help'.)

Evaluation: Very small sample so unreliable; cannot generalise to females/ other sports. Controls allow high confidence in results being due to IV. Ethical issues.
Debates: Social determinism/situational explanations of behaviour (expectancy effects). Useful to convince athletes of the power of the mind (link – cognitive techniques) and to dissuade from taking performance-enhancing drugs.

Exam tip
Link – personality
(e.g. perfectionism).

Results: Trial 1: All lifters achieved weights equal to or within 2.5 kg of their personal best (confirming diet/training unlikely to impact on subsequent performance results). Trial 2: All reported increased vigour, lifting heavier weights/ completing more repetitions than previous bests. Performance results shown in Table 12.3 below.

▼ **Table 12.3** Mean changes from baseline lifts (by group) in kg (+ increase, – decrease)

Group	Bench		Deadlift		Squat	
	Trial 1	Trial 2	Trial 1	Trial 2	Trial 1	Trial 2
AS/AS	+8.7	+9.2	+10.8	+10.8	+12.5	+11.7
AS/P	+10.5	+4.5	+11.5	-1.5	+11.5	0

Improved performance 'with AS' was confirmed in both groups from Trial 1 (and AS/AS, Trial 2). AS/P reduced performance on Trial 2 confirms (negative) expectancy.

No significant changes found in nutrition and body mass data (monitored throughout) – supports interpretation that performance changes were due to expectancy effects.

appropriate items; revised scale included 12 items. New sample completed this scale and a second was obtained for replication purposes.

SPAS example items:
1. I am comfortable with the appearance of my physique/figure.
9. It would make me uncomfortable to know others were evaluating my physique/figure.

Study 2: Constuct Validation. Participants completed SPAS, four other related measures and a social desirability scale (Reynolds, 1982).
Study 3: Criterion-related validation. Women who scored either high or low on SPAS were compared during their physique evaluation. Participants weighed, interviewed, had body fat measured (skinfold callipers) and completed an 11-point Likert scale assessing how stressed they felt during evaluation, etc., and selected figure from drawings which best characterised their own physique.

Evaluation: Extensive procedure for piloting, checking validity and reliability means we can have high confidence in the SPAS as a measure. Large samples reliable; however, age restriction means cannot generalise to older age groups.
Debates: Useful to enable support of anxious individuals who may want/need to engage in exercise. Social determinism/situational explanations of behaviour. Reductionist – does not investigate pre-existing fitness levels (women shot-putters typically 'heavy'). Differing cultural norms (ideal body type) means it would be ethnocentric to apply findings.

METHODS OF DATA COLLECTION AND ANALYSIS

▲ **Figure 13.1** Questionnaires are a self-report method

The experimental method

Psychology has for over a century regarded itself as a science. This means that the empirical evidence on which psychologists base their conclusions is generally collected according to the rules of scientific enquiry. The scientific method is based upon deduction. This means that scientists come up with theories and then they carry out investigations in order to obtain objective data that disprove or support their theories.

Experiments should all obey the same set of rules:

- **Theory:** The aim of an experiment is to test a hypothesis (predictions) with the aim of disproving or supporting it.

- **Test:** In order to test the prediction, it has to be established that one variable (thing) has a measurable effect on another variable (thing).

The observational method

The observational method is one of the most important data collection methods available to psychologists. This is particularly true of social psychologists as their aim is to study human interactions and group behaviours, which are normally observable.

- In an observation, data are collected by someone observing (watching) participants and recording (taking notes of) what the participants do and say.

- Sometimes the observer is present (overt) and sometimes the observer is hidden (covert) behind a one-way mirror (a window that looks like a mirror from the participants' viewpoint).

- Other recording techniques can be used, including video recordings and CCTV footage.

- Observations may be conducted on their own or they may be conducted as part of an experiment.

Correlation

Correlation differs from the previous research methods in that it is not a method of data collection but a data analysis technique. It is used in studies that are not experimental, i.e. cause and effect cannot be established. It enables relationships between variables to be established but not cause and effect.

- Correlation is a data analysis technique, not a method of data collection.
- Correlations are relationships between variables.
- Correlations can be positive or negative.
- When a correlation is positive, the values of one variable increase as the values of the other variable increase.
- When a correlation is negative the values of one variable decrease as the values of the other variable increase.
- Correlations are shown by drawing scattergraphs which show the relationship between participants' scores/measurements on both variables.

- **Control:** The study must be conducted under controlled conditions so that the researcher can identify that the effect that has been found is due only to an identified variable and not to other factors that were not tested.

- **Replication:** In order for support for a theory to be retested it is vital that any experiment can be replicated (imitated with the same results) by others. This means that the method must be identified precisely and be standardised so that it can be imitated. If the experiment is copied by others with the same or similar results then we say that it has been replicated.

Self-report

Self-report is a method of data collection in which the participant answers questions about their behaviour, thoughts or feelings. Questions may be asked in an interview or in the form of a questionnaire that participants are asked to respond to.

- Instead of using an objective method of data collection, participants are asked to make subjective judgements.
- Interviews are a commonly used technique in clinical psychology and psychotherapy. They can be structured, semi-structured or unstructured.
- Usually self-report questions are responded to by participants themselves, although occasionally others respond for them, e.g. in the case of small children or people with learning difficulties who are unable to respond on their own behalf.
- As with observations, self-report is a method in its own right, but it is also frequently incorporated into experiments.
- The most common form of self-report in psychological investigations is the questionnaire or psychological measure.
- Questionnaires can have open or closed questions. Open questions are open ended and allow free reign in answering them, while closed questions only allow participants a certain range of answers.
- Questionnaires frequently use a rating scale. They can consist of questions or statements which participants respond to on a scale (e.g. a Likert scale) where responses may take the form of 'strongly disagree' to 'strongly agree' on a scale of 1–4 where 1 = strongly disagree and 4 = strongly agree.

STRENGTHS AND WEAKNESSES OF RESEARCH METHODS

Strengths of experiments

✔ Experiments enable you to test hypotheses by manipulation of an independent variable.

✔ Experiments are scientific as they follow standardised procedures which enable replication.

✔ Experiments enable the researcher to control extraneous variables, thereby improving reliability of results.

✔ Experiments normally produce quantitative data that can be subjected to statistical analysis, which ensures that results of different groups of participants can be meaningfully compared.

Weaknesses of experiments

✘ Experiments are often low in ecological validity as they are generally controlled situations removed from real life.

✘ Experiments are difficult to organise in practical terms as you have to run them in controlled conditions and this means sample sizes are usually small, thus reducing generalizability.

✘ Participating in experiments, especially if run in laboratories, may cause anxiety or stress in participants, particularly children or vulnerable adults, and this is a problem in terms of ethics.

✘ Experiments do not normally involve collection of qualitative data such as people's feelings as they participate, which means that the results are generally reduced to numerical data such as scores.

Strengths of observations

✔ Observations are often high in ecological validity as they are generally conducted in naturalistic environments.

✔ Observations normally produce rich data. They may produce quantitative data that can be subjected to statistical analysis, but they can also produce qualitative data that can give some insight into people's reactions and feelings in relation to particular events.

✔ Observations are comparatively easy to run in practical terms as you do not need to advertise for participants or disturb participants from their day-to-day activities if they are run in a natural environment.

✔ Observations are often low in demand characteristics as people are usually unaware they are being observed.

Weaknesses of observation

✘ Observations do not enable you to assess cause and effect unless they are part of a controlled experiment.

✘ Observations are often covert, which raises ethical issues as participants are not aware that they are being observed or that they are taking part in an investigation. There is normally no opportunity either for informed consent or for debriefing.

✘ In observations it is generally not possible to control variables, which means that there is little standardisation and they can be hard to replicate.

✘ Overt observations are not subject to the same ethical issues as covert observations, but they raise the problem of demand characteristics as people will not behave normally if they know they are being watched.

Strengths of self-report

✔ Self-report is a valuable method of investigating thoughts and feelings that cannot be investigated using other methods.

✔ Self-report is a practical research method that enables investigators to collect large quantities of data quickly when the questionnaire method is used.

✔ Self-report measures are usually standardised and easily reproduced, enabling studies to be replicated.

✔ Self-report data can produce numerical data that can be analysed using statistical methods.

Weaknesses of self-report

✘ Self-report is a subjective method of data collection that is not subject to scientific scrutiny.

✘ Interviewing can be time-consuming and is not normally conducted on large samples.

✘ It is not possible to gauge whether respondents are telling the truth in their responses.

✘ If self-report responses require respondents to recall events or feelings, their responses can be affected by reliability issues.

▲ **Figure 13.2** Laboratory experiments allow control of extraneous variables but may lack ecological validity

Strengths of correlational analysis

✔ Correlation is a useful tool in psychology as it allows us to measure the relationship between variables which it would be difficult or unethical to manipulate experimentally. For example, we might be interested in investigating the relationship between reported stress and ill health. It would be impractical and unethical to manipulate stress or health. However, it is possible to correlate self-reported levels of stress with health data in order to establish whether there is a relationship between the two.

Weaknesses of correlational analysis

✘ The major problem with correlational evidence is that correlation does not imply causation. In other words, just because two variables are correlated does not mean that one of them has caused the other to change.

Research questions

You may be asked to formulate your own research question in response to source material. A research question is a question that a researcher poses that they wish to investigate. It should clearly relate to the aim of the project as conveyed by the source material.

Follow these steps in formulating your research question to avoid the traps students often fall in to. A research question must:

● be framed as a question, not a statement

● include all the wording of the source material

● be clear and appropriate.

Framing operationalised hypotheses

You might be asked to state and operationalise a null hypothesis. Remember that the null hypothesis in an experiment is that there will be no effect of the independent variable (IV) on the dependent variable (DV). Another way of expressing the null hypothesis is that there will be no difference in results between the two conditions of the IV. Alternatively, you might be asked to operationalise the alternate and null hypotheses.

When you formulate any hypothesis (null or alternate) in the exam you are expected to operationalise it, even if the question does not explicitly mention this. To do this you must:

● explain how you plan to manipulate your IV – so you must clearly describe both conditions of your experiment

● explain exactly how your DV will be measured or scored.

You might also be asked to indicate whether the alternate hypothesis is one-tailed or two-tailed. A one-tailed hypothesis predicts the direction of change of the DV in reaction to manipulation of the IV. A two-tailed hypothesis predicts that there will be a change in the DV given manipulation of the IV but does not specify the direction of this change.

Remember a null hypothesis does not have any tails as it specifies that there will be no change in the DV.

Experimental design

There are three main experimental designs:

- **Independent measures**: In an independent measures design participants are randomly allocated to groups and each group is tested in one condition.
- **Repeated measures**: In a repeated measures design the same participants are tested in two or more conditions. The means obtained in each condition are then calculated and mean difference between conditions is calculated. If a significant difference is found, this supports the experimental hypothesis. If no significant difference is found, the null hypothesis is retained.
- **Matched participants**: In a matched participants design, participants are divided into groups on the basis of matching on one or more criteria such as age, gender, verbal ability, etc.

One experimental design is not better than another. However, one design is usually better suited to a particular investigation than another. When choosing an experimental design you need to evaluate what each offers in the context of your study. Table 13.1 outlines the main strengths and weaknesses of each design, but these should be considered only in the light of particular studies.

▼ **Table 13.1** Evaluation of different types of experimental design

	Strengths	**Weaknesses**
Independent measures	• No order effects as participants participate in the experiment once only • Demand characteristics are reduced as the participants participate in the experiment once only	• Even with random allocation of participants to groups it is not possible to control participant variables effectively because sample size is normally small
Repeated measures	• Removes participant variables as each participant is tested in both/all conditions	• Order effects need to be controlled • There is less control of task variables as different materials need to be presented each time in order to remove order effects • There is a greater likelihood of demand characteristics because participants go through the procedure more than once
Matched participants	• Extraneous variables are well controlled	• It is impossible to control all extraneous variables so in practice participants are normally matched on only one or two variables

There are also quasi- or natural experiments where participants cannot be randomly allocated to an experimental condition (for example, testing differences between males and females, or Aspergers or Tourette's Syndrome participants).

SAMPLING

Overview

Once a researcher has decided on the hypothesis that they wish to test and the design and procedure of their planned study, the next step is to obtain participants. This is referred to as obtaining the sample. The sample is the participants. There can be as few as one participant or as many as thousands in the sample. The sample can be composed of one, two or several different groups. You will probably have seen participants referred to as 'subjects' in some of the studies you have come across. Usually these are studies that were conducted some time ago and it is now regarded as more ethically sound to use the term 'participant'.

There are different ways in which researchers can obtain their sample. The method they choose is dependent on the nature and aim of the proposed study and practical concerns, such as time constraints and whether characteristics of the sample (for example gender or being diagnosed with a clinical condition) are part of the study or not.

Although there are several different ways in which participants can be obtained for a study, the three main ways that you need to know about at A2 Level are:

1. Opportunity sample
2. Random sample
3. Self-selected (volunteer) sample.

Opportunity sample

An opportunity sample is one composed of participants who happen to be in the right place at the right time for your research. Although not highly regarded as a sampling method (because it is unlikely to be representative), this is probably the most common method that psychologists use to obtain a sample. This is because it is often the easiest way of obtaining participants and for some research (e.g. field experiments, some observations) it is the only way to obtain a sample.

Much psychological research that uses opportunity sampling is based on undergraduate psychology students who are always available to researchers and often have to participate in research for course credits. Unfortunately, this means that much interesting research cannot be generalised beyond this population. Remember, even when you use an opportunity sample, informed consent should always be obtained prior to participation unless you are conducting a covert observation.

▲ Figure 13.3

Random sample

This is the method that is most highly regarded in psychology but is in practice rarely used. The aim of random sampling is that you gain a truly representative sample of participants from a particular population of interest. This is achievable in small populations, for example randomly selecting A Level students from your school or college, but with larger populations this becomes more difficult.

It may be that some of the participants you selected for your random sample do not want

to take part, or are unable to. In this case your random sample begins to lose validity – no longer being a genuinely random sample.

▼ Table 13.2 Strengths and weaknesses of sampling techniques

Sampling method	Strength	Weakness
Opportunity	Easy to obtain	Often not representative, though can be if large and carefully obtained
Random	The most representative sampling method	Very difficult to obtain unless the target population is limited
Self-selected	Ethically sound as all participants have volunteered	Very unlikely to be representative and difficult to obtain in large numbers

Self-selecting (volunteer) sample

Self-selecting sampling is probably the second most commonly used method of obtaining a sample for psychology research after opportunity sampling. The difference between an opportunity sample and a self-selecting sample is that whereas in the former case the experimenter approaches a possible participant and asks them if they would be willing to participate in their study, in a self-selecting sample the experimenter simply publicises the study in appropriate places/ways and waits for people to put themselves forward as participants.

Obtaining such a sample can be done in many ways. Traditional methods are using posters and leaflets to advertise a project and ask for volunteers. However, where you place your publicity is an issue. If you advertise in a college or university, your volunteers will almost certainly be students. Other possible methods include approaching local firms or GP surgeries (family doctors) and asking them to ask for volunteers from their workforce/patients. This enables a higher degree of targeting of the sort of population you are hoping to obtain volunteers from. Other methods are to advertise in newspapers and magazines or on local radio stations. A very common method nowadays to obtain a self-selected sample for a questionnaire study is to use the email system of large organisations. You could also use social network sites such as Facebook.

The main issue with self-selecting samples is the motivation of the participants for volunteering. It is usually because they have a particular interest in the focus of the project you are conducting.

PROCEDURE

Overview

For G544, the term 'procedure' refers to all the steps that you take in designing and conducting an investigation. For the purpose of the examination you are expected to include an answer to questions about 'procedure' details of the design of your investigation and how you obtained your sample. Procedures followed in research practicals depend entirely on the nature of the project. There is no 'one size fits all' approach in conducting a study. However, although details of procedures are method- and context-dependent, there are some basic common factors that can be identified:

▼ Table 13.3

	Experiment	Observation	Self-report
1	Decide aim, research question and alternate/null hypotheses	Decide aim and research question	Decide aim and research question
2	Plan procedure, including obtaining ethics approval, choosing experimental design, operationalising the hypothesis, preparation of materials and deciding sampling method	Plan procedure; obtain ethics approval, draw up schedule (if structured observation); choose and train observers; plan time and location for observation	Plan procedure; obtain ethics approval, decide sampling method; construct questionnaire or draw up interview questions
3	Obtain sample and make arrangement for conduct of study	Possibly run pilot study in order to check on usefulness of selected categories and feasibility	Organise distribution of self-report measure or organise interviews (if interview study)
4	Obtain informed consent from participants	Covert observation – no informed consent/overt observation – participants informed that observation will be conducted	Obtain informed consent from participants (usually done at same time as next step)
5	Allocate participants to experimental conditions and give instructions	Place observers in position	Distribute questionnaire
6	Participants follow experimental steps (data collected)	Conduct observation – participants are observed for designated period while observers record behaviours (data collected)	Participants respond to questionnaire (data collected)
7	Thank and debrief participants	Thank and debrief participants (overt observation)	Thank and debrief participants
8	Analyse data, produce findings and draw conclusions	Analyse data, produce findings and draw conclusions	Analyse data, produce findings and draw conclusions
9	Write report of practical investigation	Write report of practical investigation	Write report of practical investigation

Confounding and extraneous variables

Closely related to the issue of reliability and validity of measurement is the issue of extraneous and confounding variables. These are not quite synonymous (they mean almost but not quite the same thing), but for our purposes we can treat them as the same. We use the term 'confounding' as that expresses the idea that this other thing has messed up (confounded) our results. When we use the term 'extraneous' this conveys the idea that this other thing is one outside of our control and may have had some effect on the results without necessarily negating the results. In practice, both confounding and extraneous variable have the same effect – they reduce the reliability of our results and hence the validity of the study.

In psychological investigations it is important to take account of extraneous variables and to control them as far as possible.

Order effects, practice effects and boredom effects

In a repeated measures design there are factors that need to be considered that might affect the reliability of the results. These include order effects, practice effects and boredom effects.

Order effects – When participants are asked to undertake the same or a very similar task in two conditions (e.g. in the morning and the afternoon) the order in which the tasks are presented may affect the results. For example, if participants are given two different word lists to memorise in the morning and the afternoon and they remember more correctly in the morning, this may be as a result of the manipulation of the IV (morning/afternoon) or it might be because the morning list is easier than the afternoon list. The order of presentation of the lists is therefore important. It is best if you can counter order effects by giving half the children one list (list A) in the morning and half the other list (list B) in the morning and then swapping round.

Practice effects – Practice effects can operate in a similar way to order effects. If you give children two word lists to memorise in the morning and the afternoon, they may do better in the afternoon simply because the first time was like a practice and so results would be affected by their level of expertise. Practice effects are more difficult to control for than order effects. Again, you can counterbalance by having half the children do the task first in the morning and half do the task first in the afternoon and swapping round, but this means that it will take two days to complete the study rather than one.

Boredom effects – Boredom is a factor that could operate in the opposite direction to practice effects. If children are given word lists in both the morning and the afternoon they may try their best in the morning, but they may be bored the second time around and not try so hard. If you use the same method as suggested for practice effects it should be possible to control for boredom effects as well as practice effects.

CASE STUDIES AND LONGITUDINAL AND SNAPSHOT DESIGNS

Case studies

In addition to the four research methods discussed on pages 88–91, which you will recognise from your AS course, there is an additional method you must know about at A2, the case study.

A case study is an in-depth study of one participant or a small group of participants, often carried out over an extended period of time (longitudinally). Within the case study method a number of different data-gathering techniques can be used. For example, recorded interviews, case notes (of therapeutic interviews, for example), observation and psychometric tests.

Strengths of case studies

✔ The case study is useful in describing atypical, abnormal or rare behaviour. In abnormal psychology the case study is seen as a useful way of exploring a participant's past experiences to help them deal with current difficulties.

✔ The data gathered is usually qualitative and rich in detail, so can be highly valid. The bond of trust that can be built up between researcher and participant also means that the data is more likely to be valid than if the researcher were a stranger having only one interview with the participant.

Weaknesses of case studies

✗ The close bond between researcher and participant can also be a weakness, as the researcher may lose their objectivity. Their interpretations of data may also be affected by biases formed as a result of their long-term investment in the project.

✗ Replication of case studies is not usually possible, particularly where a therapeutic approach has been taken. This makes it difficult to establish the reliability of findings.

✗ Generalising from the findings of case studies can be difficult, as the cases selected for study are often unusual or even unique.

✗ Case studies can be costly in terms of both time and money.

Longitudinal design

A case study often takes place over a long period of time and would therefore be a longitudinal study.

In a longitudinal study, one subject or participant or one group of individuals is studied over a long period of time, for example, taking periodic samples of behaviour. This design allows us to track development and enables us to monitor changes over time.

Snapshot design

In a snapshot design, different groups of people are tested at the same point in time and their performances compared.

The advantages that snapshot studies have over longitudinal studies is that they are relatively quick and inexpensive to carry out, can be easily replicated to test the reliability of findings and are relatively easy to modify. This final point means that if design faults become apparent, the study can be repeated with modifications to eliminate them. It also means that variations of the study can be easily carried out to investigate fully the variables that may affect behaviour.

LEVELS OF MEASUREMENT

Overview

There are four different kinds of scales or levels of measurement of data:

- nominal
- ordinal
- interval
- ratio.

Ordinal data

If the practical project that you are asked to design is an experiment or a correlation it is likely that the source material will state that you need to collect 'at least ordinal data'. Ordinal data involves numbers that can be put in order but do not have any other mathematical properties. For example, viewers of X Factor might be asked to rank the top ten finalists in their preferred order, with their favourite being ranked 10. This would give each finalist a number, but there would be no reality to those numbers. The finalist ranked top (1) would not be measurably twice as popular as the finalist ranked 5. In psychological research most studies that use self-report collect ordinal data as participants are often asked to rank things on a scale of 1–5, but the numbers stand for words such as 'strongly agree' or 'disagree' and do not have any true mathematical relationship to each other. The reason that the source material may ask for 'at least ordinal data' is that ordinal data allow you to calculate measures of central tendency (averages) and measures of dispersion.

Nominal data

In nominal data the number is just a label or name for a category that does not have any mathematical properties. For example, you might conduct research to see whether males and females who go into a shop come out with a bag showing that they have purchased an item. This can be coded using the numbers 1 (for having made no purchase) and 2 (having made a purchase). You can calculate purchasing frequency for each gender from your nominal data, but the numbers themselves are simply an easy way of coding behaviours.

Interval-level data

While the ranks ascribed in ordinal-level data have no true mathematical relationship, interval-level data are data in which the points are evenly spaced. For example, the difference between shoe size 3 and shoe size 4 is the same as between shoe size 4 and shoe size 5. However, there is no zero in shoe sizes so the relationship is relative.

Ratio data

Ratio data are the highest, most precise level of measurement. Unlike interval-level data, zero truly means zero. Often interval and ratio data are grouped together and the question will ask for 'at least interval-level data'. These include physiological measures such as height and weight, but in psychology they also include measures such as scores on an IQ test, number of words remembered in a memory test or time taken to complete a task.

ETHICAL ISSUES

Overview

A top priority of researchers in any field that deals with human participants is to ensure that they conform to high ethical standards. The ethical code by which British psychologists work today (*Code of Ethics and Conduct,* British Psychological Society, 2009) is much stricter than guidelines in the past.

Avoidance of psychological harm

It is essential that any research conducted by psychologists and psychology students does not cause psychological harm to participants. This means that studies should avoid presenting participants with tasks or scenarios that might induce unpleasant emotions or states of mind such as anxiety, fear, stress, unhappiness, nor must they expose participants to any physical risk.

There are several ways of dealing with this issue, for example debriefing participants thoroughly at the end of the study, with the aim of restoring them to the state of mind they were before they began and reassuring them that their data will be kept confidential. Also informing them of exactly what will be involved in the study before they take part, and letting them know they can withdraw at any time.

Informed consent

The British Psychological Society guidelines require that where practicable researchers should always obtain informed consent from participants prior to starting. This means that participants should be given information about what they will be asked to do during the study and they should confirm verbally or in writing that they understand the study and are willing to participate. In the case of children, parental consent should be obtained in advance and the children themselves should be asked for their assent – that is to say, whether they are happy to continue. In practice, when researchers carry out studies in schools in the UK, the school normally informs parents in writing of the possibility that research may be carried out with their child, and asks them to inform the school if they wish their child to be withdrawn from any such research studies. Asking individuals to opt out rather than opt in ensures higher numbers of participants while still offering parents the right of informed consent.

It is permitted to conduct unobtrusive observations in public places without asking for consent, as long as you are discreet and do not approach or identify people as individuals.

Deception

Information given to participants (or the parents of child participants) does not have to include the exact aims of the investigation, but at the same time it should not be deceptive.
Sometimes telling participants the exact purpose or nature of an experiment would negate the results of that experiment, resulting in behaviour that is unnatural. In these cases a full debriefing at the conclusion of the experiment and the opportunity to withdraw their data should be offered.

Right to withdraw

During the introduction to the study when informed consent is obtained the researcher must tell participants that they have the right to withdraw, and the right to not answer any question at any time. Particular attention should be given to ensuring that children understand that they can ask to stop at any time.

Confidentiality/anonymity

Individual participants should not be identified or identifiable in any write-up of the study, nor should the participants discuss individuals' performance with anyone.

▲ **Figure 13.4** Researchers must not expose participants to physical or psychological harm

Debrief

Debriefing is not an ethical issue, it is a way of addressing ethical issues. At the end of the study participants should be made aware of the real aims of the study and should be given the opportunity to ask questions of the researchers. This is called the debrief. During the debrief participants should be given the opportunity to ask for the results of the study if it is published and they should be informed that any discussion or publication of the study will ensure anonymity of participants.

DATA COLLECTION AND RECORDING

Overview

A psychological investigation will collect data which can be qualitative or quantitative. Once you have your data it is important you know how to present, summarise and describe the findings. You must know about descriptive statistics, which help describe the data but do not test its statistical significance and you must know about graphical representations of data, for example graphs and charts.

Qualitative data

Qualitative data are data that are not numerical. They are descriptive data. They can be a rich source of information on behaviours and attitudes. In order to draw meaningful conclusions from qualitative data, it is usually necessary to impose structure on the raw data. For example, content analysis can be used to analyse texts or interviews for common themes.

- A strength of qualitative data is that they are not limited by preselected categories and therefore enable full description of behaviour, feelings or attitudes.

- A weakness of qualitative data is that they can be difficult to analyse and make comparisons or draw meaningful conclusions.

Quantitative data

Most psychological investigations today collect quantitative data. Quantitative data are numerical data (e.g. scores on tests) that can be analysed statistically in order to provide comparisons between groups of participants or to show statistically meaningful relationships between variables. One of the reasons that quantitative data are commonly collected today is that sophisticated computer programs enable vast quantities of numerical data to be analysed according to a variety of methods. However, it is still important to understand the statistical principles that such computer programs employ. In particular it should be noted that the results are reliable only if the data collection and inputting are done correctly and the appropriate statistical test is applied.

- A strength of quantitative data is that they allow statistical analysis, enabling cause and effect to be measured and relationships between variables to be analysed.

- A weakness of quantitative data is that they can impose limited choices on participants and by imposing categories can miss out on potentially important aspects of behaviour or feelings.

Measures of dispersion – the range

As well as being able to summarise a set of scores by looking at central, average or typical scores, it is useful to know how widely dispersed or spread out the scores are. To calculate the range of a set of scores you simply subtract the lowest score in the set from the highest score.

Measures of central tendency

A measure of central tendency refers to one numerical value that best represents the data (an average). This can be the mean, median or mode. In order to gain a fuller understanding of the spread of your data, a measure of dispersion (e.g. range) is also frequently calculated.

Mean

The mean is calculated by adding together all the values in the dataset and dividing by the number of values. For measuring things such as time, or weight or height or anything where decimal accuracy has real meaning, the mean average is usually the best and most accurate measure of central tendency to work with. However, there is a problem with the mean, as it can give us what is called 'spurious accuracy'. This means that in some circumstances the mean can produce a value which does not represent any of the actual data values. For this reason it is sometimes better to use an alternative measure of central tendency, the median or the mode.

Median

There are two circumstances in which the median can be a more useful measure of central tendency than the mean. The first is when you are measuring whole numbers such as scores on a rating scale. The other is when you have a combination of a relatively small set of scores and one score that is very high or low and therefore distorts or skews the mean. The median identifies the central point of a set of scores. The median is worked out by putting all the scores in size order and finding the central point. If there is an even number of scores in the set you take a mean of the middle two scores to find the median.

Mode

There are instances, however, when the median is not particularly representative of the data we are analysing. If you have a small set of scores and one score clearly predominates, it may be better to calculate the mode. This simply tells us the most frequently occurring value in the set. The mode will always represent at least two scores in the actual set of scores, but loses its meaningfulness if there are more than two modes. Of course, if each score occurs only once in a set then there is no mode, so this measure of central tendency is not useful where all items are different in the set.

Graphical representations of data

Bar charts

Bar charts are a useful and meaningful way of presenting summarised data from an experiment. Bar charts should not show scores of individual participants but should be drawn based on a measure of central tendency for each condition (normally the mean) and bars should be drawn to show calculated difference between the two conditions.

You might also be asked to draw conclusions from data presented in a bar graph. As long as you read carefully the axis labels, the title and any key, this should be straightforward.

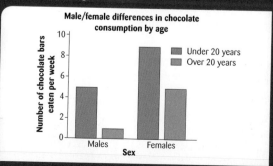

▲ **Figure 13.5** Example of a bar chart

Correlations

You might also be asked to draw a scattergraph in response to correlational data, or to interpret data presented in scattergraph format.

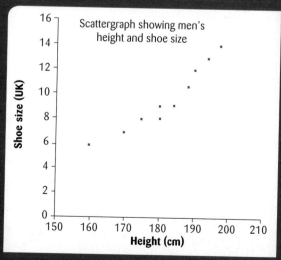

▲ **Figure 13.6** Correlational data could be used to draw a scattergraph

DATA ANALYSIS

Overview

One aspect of data handling in Unit G544 is inferential statistics. This might sound intimidating but the examiners will not expect you to be able to actually carry out the tests, although you should understand their purpose and you may be asked to indicate in relation to designing a procedure which test you would carry out and why.

Inferential tests are simply tests that enable us to conclude that a difference we have found between

Types of inferential test

There are five statistical tests that you need to know about. These are all non-parametric tests. This means that they are tests for data that are not normally distributed.

▼ Table 13.4 Non-parametric inferential tests and their use

Test	When to use the test
Chi-square test	This is used for nominal data when data are categorical. You can have a two-by-two or a three-by-two chi square test
Sign test	This is used for ordinal data when you are looking for a difference between conditions and your design is repeated measures. Usually the Wilcoxon is preferred
Wilcoxon signed-ranks test	This is used for ordinal- or interval-level data and is used when you are looking for a difference between two conditions and when your experimental design is either repeated measures or matched pairs
Mann-Whitney U test	This is used for ordinal- or interval-level data when you are looking for a difference between two conditions and your experimental design is independent measures
Spearman's rho rank correlation coefficient	This is a test of relationship (correlation) and can be used for ordinal- or interval-level data and measures relationships between variables for each participant

Probability

What you need to know for G544 is how in psychological research probability is expressed and at what level of probability researchers would agree that a finding is not due to chance.

The probability of a difference between groups being due to chance is expressed as $p \leq 0.05$. This means there is 5% or lower probability that the differences are due to chance factors and that there is a 95% or higher probability that the differences are due to the effect of the manipulation of the IV.

At this point we can accept that the difference is significant, which means we can reject the null hypothesis and accept the alternate hypothesis. Sometimes psychology researchers want to set a more stringent level of significance, in which case they will set the level at $p \leq 0.01$. This means that the probability that the difference is due to chance factors is only 1% or less and the probability that the finding is due to manipulation of the IV is 99% or higher.

In the examination you will not have to work out levels of significance but you may need to show that you understand them. For example, you may be asked to explain what is meant by the statement 'the researchers set the probability level at $p \leq 0.05$'.

scores of different groups of participants is meaningful (statistically significant) or whether the differences were at a level that may have occurred by chance. An inferential test helps us to decide by working out the probability of whether the difference between the two sets of scores is due to chance or a real effect.

Type 1 and Type 2 errors

Normally we can be confident in accepting the alternate hypothesis when there is a 5% or lower probability of results having occurred by chance. However, we are dealing with probabilities, not with certainties, and sometimes mistakes are made. If we accidentally accept the alternate hypothesis wrongly, this may mean that we have not operated a stringent enough measure of probability. This is a false positive or Type 1 error.

If, however, we reject the alternate hypothesis and wrongly accept the null hypothesis, this means that we have operated too stringent a level of probability and the result is a false negative or Type 2 error (see Table 13.5).

▼ **Table 13.5** Type 1 and Type 2 errors

Type 1 error	False positive	Accepting the alternate hypothesis although the null was true
Type 2 error	False negative	Accepting the null hypothesis although the alternate was true

Usually it is important in psychological research that we do not claim the alternate hypothesis is true if it is not (a false positive) and that is why psychologists sometimes operate on more stringent levels of probability ($p \leq 0.01$).

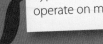

VALIDITY AND RELIABILITY

Overview

Reliability and validity are the two concepts students find the most confusing concerning psychological investigations. Reliability means the consistency of the measure, the ability of someone else to repeat the study and get the same results, while validity means whether the measure actually measures what the researchers want it to.

Reliability

Reliability refers to the consistency of a measurement. A test or measure is reliable if it gives similar results when carried out again in similar circumstances. In other words, if the findings prove to be replicable (consistent) when the same or a similar researcher carries out the study again, the test or measure is reliable. If the study is not reliable, that is, if the repeat of the study gives different results from the original, this gives us reason to question the validity of the original research. Reliable findings can help to support the validity of research.

Inter-observer reliability

In order to avoid observer bias (i.e. an observer applying ratings or counting categories in a subjective rather than objective fashion), inter-observer reliability needs to be established. This means that two observers rate or observe the same behaviour, and the two sets of ratings are correlated. If a significant positive correlation is seen, inter-observer reliability has been established and the objectivity of the results is confirmed.

Validity

When we ask, 'Are the findings of a study valid?', what we are really asking is, 'Can we trust the findings? Are there any reasons to believe that they might not be true?'

Face validity

A study has face validity if it answers the question the experimenter wants answered. If the measure used is also reliable then we can probably draw the conclusion that it is valid.

Internal validity (design validity)

Internal validity is determined by the extent to which a study is free of design faults which might affect the result, meaning that the test is not a true test of what it intended to measure. Factors which reduce the validity (internal validity) of findings include the following:

- Low generalisability of findings (e.g. sample biases, ethnocentric bias, difficulty extrapolating to other groups of people or settings). If the findings are not generalisable, they are not valid.
- If demand characteristics might have affected the study.
- If the findings of the study do not prove to be reliable.
- If it is possible that a confounding variable has operated systematically alongside the independent variable this might affect the validity of the findings.
- If it is possible that the study is out of date or has lost validity over time. This is a particular problem for studies in social psychology. Social, political, cultural and technological changes can mean that a study only represents the time and place in which it was carried out. We cannot generalise the findings to the present day.

Ecological validity

Is the behaviour that the participants are being asked to perform in the study comparable with behaviours that people might carry out in the course of their everyday life? In other words, how realistic is the study? If the behaviour in a study is very like real-life behaviours, the study is said to be high in ecological validity. If the behaviours required of participants in a study are not like real-life behaviours, the study is low in ecological validity and this limits its usefulness.

APPROACHES IN PSYCHOLOGY

Overview

Each of the approaches focuses on a different explanation of human behaviour. Human behaviour is complex, and so different approaches look at different aspects of it and try to offer useful explanations for specific behaviours. Each of the approaches, then, make different assumptions about human behaviour, and this will have an impact on which aspects of behaviour

The social approach

The social approach assumes that our behaviour is not always the result of our own free will. The situation we are in will have a strong influence on how we behave. For example, the presence of a legitimate authority figure can override our individual conscience, or our group identity can have more impact on our behaviour than our individual personalities. An assumption of the social approach is that situational rather than individual explanations of social behaviour are often more accurate as context and culture has a strong influence on how we behave.

Weaknesses of the social approach

✗ One limitation of the social approach is that studying social behaviour under laboratory conditions can be problematic since subjects or participants may not behave in a typical or naturalistic way.

✗ The use of field experiments in the social approach can also make it difficult to study social behaviour because it is difficult to control extraneous variables in a field setting. This means that studies may lack validity because we cannot be sure that extraneous variables have not confounded them.

✗ Social approach studies can raise ethical concerns. To try to stop behaviour being affected by subject reactivity, deception is often needed. This means that the researcher must carefully weigh up whether the study justifies breaching the ethical guidelines.

✗ Social approach studies can lose validity over time, as social or cultural changes mean that the study's findings may go out of date.

✗ Social behaviour can be difficult to measure. What this means is that the findings lack ecological validity and cannot easily be generalised to a real life setting, and this problem can limit the usefulness of social approach studies.

Strengths of the social approach

✔ It can provide information to explain how other people, such as authority figures or people we see as being in the same group as ourselves, have an effect on our behaviour and how social cognition influences our social behaviour. Such insights into behaviour mean that the social approach makes an important contribution to psychology as a discipline.

✔ It often uses field experiments to study social behaviour. This enables researchers to study how people behave in naturalistic settings. This means that the studies often have high ecological validity and can explain how people behave in real-life settings as opposed to how they behave in the artificial setting of the laboratory.

The cognitive approach

The cognitive approach focuses on how information received from our senses is processed by our brains. This approach assumes that how we process information, including how we perceive, store and retrieve information, influences how we behave.

The cognitive approach assumes that we can and should study mental processes such as memory, ways of thinking and problem solving in order to further understand human behaviour. It assumes that these mental processes can be studied scientifically, so the experimental method is favoured by cognitive psychologists in their research.

The cognitive approach uses a computer analogy to describe how the brain processes information, assuming that comparisons can be made between how machines process information and how brains process information.

researchers working within an approach choose to study, and on the methods researchers use to investigate behaviour. Each contributes to psychology and when we consider them together we get a good understanding of human psychology.

▲ **Figure 13.7** The invention of the computer gave psychologists new ways of thinking about the brain

Weaknesses of the cognitive approach

✗ The use of laboratory studies in the cognitive approach raises concerns about the ecological validity of the research, and this method also increases the chances of participants responding to demand characteristics in the study.

✗ At present, there are limitations to the way data is gathered in the cognitive approach. Cognitive processes can only be studied by inference, that is, we cannot study them directly — we can only gather what is going on in someone's head by recording what they can or cannot tell us (self-report) or can or cannot do (observation), or at best by making and interpreting recordings of the active parts of their brain by, for example, using MRI scans.

Strengths of the cognitive approach

✔ This approach favours the scientific method, using the laboratory experiment to investigate mental processes. This enables researchers to establish cause and effect between variables, provide objective evidence in which we can have confidence and to produce quantitative data, making it easier to test reliability. This approach brings academic credibility to psychology as a discipline.

✔ Some cognitive approach studies assume that there is continuity between the way animals, particularly primates, process information and the way humans process information. By studying animals we can understand human cognitive processes, for example, the acquisition of language. This means we can find out about human behaviour without the practical and ethical concerns that might be raised by an in-depth study of, for example, the language development of a human child.

The physiological (biological) approach

The physiological approach assumes that behaviour can be largely explained in terms of biology (e.g. genes/hormones): what is psychological is first biological. This approach assumes that psychology should study the brain, nervous system and various biological systems in an attempt to explain behaviour. According to the physiological approach, psychology should be seen as a science, to be studied in a scientific manner (usually in a laboratory), measuring variables objectively, for example, using physiological measures such as MRI scans or EEG recordings.

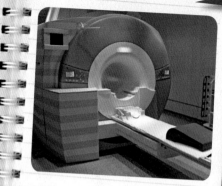

▲ **Figure 13.8** MRI scanner

The developmental approach

A major assumption of the developmental approach is that children are psychologically different from adults. In addition, some developmental approach theories assume that children's development occurs in stages, whose sequence is invariant and which are universal. Examples of this include Piaget's theory of moral development and Freud's psychosexual stages of personality development. The developmental approach assumes that children can learn through the behavioural principles of operant and classical conditioning and modelling.

Some developmental theories assume that bad early experiences can have a negative effect on us in later life, and that the root cause of adult psychiatric problems lies in problems with their psychiatric development as a child (Freud's psychodynamic theory).

Weaknesses of the developmental approach

✗ To study development you often have to study children. This raises ethical concerns because children cannot give their fully informed consent, cannot operate their right to withdraw and cannot be debriefed. It is also unethical to introduce variables that might harm the child.

✗ Another problem for the developmental approach is that there are also practical problems to be overcome when studying children. For example, when studying children in a controlled setting their behaviour may not be typical of how they would behave in a realistic social setting. They may be more vulnerable to demand characteristics.

Strengths of the developmental approach

✔ The developmental approach has furthered our understanding of the causes of behaviour. Such insights into behaviour means that the developmental approach makes an important contribution to psychology as a discipline.

✔ Another strength is that the developmental approach studies children's psychological development, not just their physical development. It has shown that children are cognitively different as well as physically different from adults and this has had a huge impact on the way we teach children in schools.

✔ One strength of the developmental approach is that it often uses the case study method to investigate development. This brings to the developmental approach the advantages associated with longitudinal research, including rich detailed data, and trust in the researcher that can lead to increased validity of the findings.

Strengths of the physiological approach

✔ The physiological approach is leading to a greater understanding of the physiognomy of the brain; we are learning how the brain works and how it impacts on our behaviour.

✔ The discipline of cognitive neuroscience is at the cutting edge of scientific enquiry and is making major contributions to our understanding of both normal and abnormal brain function.

✔ A major strength is that the physiological approach is highly scientific, grounded in biology and uses a rigorous scientific methodology in research. This means that the physiological approach brings academic credibility to psychology.

Weaknesses of the physiological approach

✘ Even though the physiological approach tries to be scientific, our limited ability to study brain processes directly and objectively means we often have to rely on self-report data, and here demand characteristics may be a problem and studies may not be entirely valid.

✘ A further problem for physiological approach studies is that studies carried out in the laboratory can be low in ecological validity.

The individual differences approach

The individual differences approach assumes that the differences between people, such as personality, abnormality or intelligence, and not just the factors that people share in common, have an important influence on our behaviour. This approach assumes that it is not only the ways we are the same as one another (the nomothetic approach in psychology, attempting to establish general rules about behaviour), but also the ways in which we differ from others and are individuals that is important for psychology to investigate. This is known as the idiographic approach.

Strengths of the individual differences approach

✔ Case studies are a popular method; they are in depth and often longitudinal studies that focus on one individual or one case. A detailed case history can be useful in describing unusual or unique cases.

✔ It recognises that individual differences are an important element of people's behaviour, something often overlooked by other approaches. By focusing on the ways people differ rather than how their behaviours fit in with general rules, the individual differences approach makes an important contribution to psychology as an academic discipline.

✔ This approach includes the study of abnormal behaviour. This is useful for helping to explain abnormal behaviour and for improving the experience of both those suffering from mental illness and those who work with them and care for them.

Weaknesses of the individual differences approach

✘ This approach often focuses on unique cases. The rarity of cases may lead to intrusive investigations and excessive study and testing, which may not help the individual and could distress them. This raises ethical concerns about the balance between the value of the research and causing possible harm to the person being investigated.

✘ There are problems with the type of data gathered in studies in the individual differences approach. In some studies in this approach large amounts of qualitative data is gathered and this can present problems for researchers as there are difficulties with its interpretation, objectivity and analysis which leads us to question its validity.

✘ Psychologists have to be careful that their findings are not misused. By focusing on the differences between people, the individual differences approach may emphasise these differences and this can lead to discrimination. Researchers in this area must present their data responsibly and be sensitive to the possible implications of highlighting differences between people.

111

PERSPECTIVES IN PSYCHOLOGY

There are two perspectives you must have an understanding of:
- the behaviourist perspective
- the psychodynamic perspective.

The behaviourist perspective

Some assumptions of the behaviourist perspective are as follows:

- The behaviourist perspective assumes that all behaviour is learned, and that learning happens through the processes of classical conditioning, operant conditioning (reinforcement) or through social learning. This means that the behaviourist perspective is at the extreme nurture end of the nature-nurture debate.

- The behaviourist perspective considers that explanations of behaviour based on internal causes or mental states are generally useless, and to study behaviour psychologists should focus only on what can be overtly observed.

- The behaviourist perspective assumes that both normal and abnormal behaviours are all learned and can be unlearned, and behaviour can be controlled and altered, not just described and quantified.

▲ **Figure 13.9** Behaviourists believe that all behaviour is learnt

Some strengths of the behaviourist perspective

✔ The behaviourist perspective highlights the role of nurture in learning, and shows the important influence environment has on our behaviour.

✔ It assumes that behaviour can be both learned and unlearned, which means we can control and change behaviour using behaviourist techniques. The behaviourist perspective therefore offers hopeful theories about the causes of behaviours and helps develop techniques to change them.

✔ In its attempt to study behaviour it favours the scientific method and laboratory experiments in particular. This focus of the behaviourist perspective on studying observable behaviour in laboratory experiments gave psychology as a discipline the scientific credibility it previously lacked.

Some weaknesses of the behaviourist perspective

✗ A weakness of the behaviourist perspective is that by favouring the laboratory experiment as a research method studies in this approach can lack ecological validity and therefore fail to resemble behaviours that people might perform in real life.

✗ Another weakness of the behaviourist perspective is that there are moral issues and ethical objections raised against the behaviourist perspective. If the principles of behaviourism can be used to control people and change their behaviour, then who should decide which behaviours should be changed and who controls the controllers?

The psychodynamic perspective

Some assumptions of the psychodynamic perspective are as follows:

- The psychodynamic perspective assumes that all behaviour has an unconscious cause, even slips of the tongue. Therefore all behaviour is determined. We have no control over our unconscious and therefore have no free will. Behaviour is motivated from the unconscious by two instinctual drives: Eros and Thanatos.

- Another assumption of the psychodynamic perspective is that the personality has three parts which reside in the unconscious called the ego, the id and the superego. The id and superego can create conflict for the ego if the desires of the id (to spend unconscious energy) are disapproved of by the moral conscience, the superego. Failure of the ego to resolve this conflict, for example, by using defence mechanisms such as repression, sublimation or denial, can lead to 'ego anxiety' which, according to the psychodynamic perspective, is the cause of mental health problems.

Some strengths of the psychodynamic perspective

✔ Freud's theory raised for the first time the importance of the unconscious mind as an influence on our feelings and behaviour, making an important contribution to our understanding of the human mind.

✔ Freud developed a psychological treatment, or talking cure, for abnormal behaviour. Although most modern therapists do not use Freudian principles, Freud's legacy is apparent in modern forms of counselling.

✔ Freud's work made the case study method popular in psychology. Case studies provide in-depth detail about a person or client's experiences, both current and in the past. The case study method remains popular in the area of abnormal psychology.

Some weaknesses of the psychodynamic perspective

✗ The greatest weakness of the psychodynamic perspective is that it is unscientific in its analysis of human behaviour. Many of the concepts central to Freud's theories are subjective and as such impossible to scientifically test. Many psychologists reject the psychodynamic perspective because the theories and concepts cannot be empirically investigated.

✗ Evidence for psychodynamic theory is taken from Freud's case studies. The main problem here is that case studies are based on studying one person in detail and the evidence is highly subjective and can be affected by researcher bias. This puts the validity of the findings into question and makes generalisations to the wider population difficult.

113

DEBATES IN PSYCHOLOGY

Reductionism and holism

Reductionism is the process of breaking down phenomena into their constituent parts. This is a process that is seen as positive in sciences like chemistry, but in psychology it is often criticised for oversimplifying human behaviour.

Holism is an approach that attempts to take into account a whole range of factors that might together explain human behaviours.

Determinism and free will

Determinism is the view that all behaviours and mental acts such as thoughts are determined by factors beyond our control.

A belief in free will is the belief that our behaviours and mental acts are the products of our own choice and will.

- Determinist explanations can be biological or environmental. Biological determinism explains behaviours in terms of biochemical factors such as hormones, genetic factors and physiological factors such as brain structure. Environmental determinism might explain behaviour in terms of factors such as upbringing, environment and experiences.

- A free will explanation emphasises that humans have the cognitive ability to make choices about their actions.

The nature—nurture debate

This debate centres on whether behaviours are innate (inborn or genetically determined), i.e. the result of nature, or whether they are acquired as a result of experience or environmental influences (nurture). Both nature and nurture can be seen as determinist because they offer no scope for the role of free will.

Psychology as science

The issue of whether psychology is a science has long been the subject of debate.

Arguments for:
- Psychologists often use the scientific method of testing hypotheses by manipulation of IVs and rigorous control of procedures.

Arguments against:
- Psychologists study human behaviour and humans cannot be investigated in the same objective way as the physical materials or forces that are investigated in sciences such as chemistry and physics.

- Psychologists are to a large degree concerned with internal mental processes that are not directly observable and therefore not open to scientific scrutiny.

Individual and situational explanations

Individual (dispositional) explanations locate the causes of behaviours in individual characteristics that may be innate or at least located in the individual's personality.

Situational explanations explain behaviours in terms of environmental factors such as family and neighbourhood or situational or circumstantial triggers such as events or the behaviours of others.

Ethnocentrism

The original meaning of ethnocentrism is a belief in the superiority of one's own group (ethnic group or culture). However, it is nowadays normally taken to mean not a belief in the superiority of one's own group but the inability to think outside one's own cultural experience and a tendency to assume that what happens in our own culture is common to other cultures. In research terms this means that psychologists sometime draw conclusions from the experience of their own culture or group and mistakenly assume it can be generalised to other groups or cultures.

Usefulness of psychological research

This is classified by OCR as a debate but it is more properly an issue and is in fact applied to questions in the alternative Section B question on research methods and issues. Usefulness of psychological research depends on both its practical applications and its intrinsic value. To have value research should be valid. To be valid research should have face validity (it should do what it sets out to do), it should be high in ecological validity, it should abide by ethical guidelines and be generalisable.

Bibliography

Forensic

Asch, S.E. (1955) Opinions and social pressure. *Scientific America*, 193 (5), 31–5.

Brunner, H.G., Nelen, M.R., van Zandvoort, P., Abeling, N.G.G.M., van Gennip, A.H., Wolters, E.C., Kulper, M.A., Ropers, H.H. and van Oost, B.A. (1993) X-linked borderline mental retardation with prominent behavioural disturbance: phenotype, genetic localization and evidence for disturbed monoamine metabolism. *American Journal of Human Genetics*, 52, 1032–9.

Cann, J. (2006) Cognitive skills programmes: impact on reducing reconviction on a sample of female offenders. *Research Development and Statistics Directorate,* Home Office Findings 276. London: Home Office.

Canter, D., Alison, L.J., Alison, E. and Wentink, N. (2004) The organised/disorganised typology of serial murder: myth or model? *Psychology, Public Policy and the Law*, 10 (3), 293–320.

Canter, D. and Heritage, R. (1990) A multivariate model of sexual offence behaviour: developments in offender profiling. *Journal of Forensic Psychiatry*, 1, 185–212. (http://eprints.hud.ac.uk/9229)

Canter, D. (1995). Criminal Shadow: *Inside the Mind of a Serial Killer**. London: Harper Collins. (*The case of John Duffy, 1994.)

Castellow, W.A., Wuensch, K.L. and Moore, C.H. (1990) Effects of physical attractiveness of the plaintiff and defendant in sexual harassment judgements. *Journal of Social Behaviour and Personality*, 5, 547–62.

Cornish, D. and Clarke, R.V.G. (2006) The rational choice perspective. In S. Henry and M. Lanier (eds.) *The Essential Criminology Reader*. Boulder, CO: Westview Press. (Cited from Newburn, T. (2007) *Criminology*, pp. 281–5. Devon: Willan Publishing.)

Cutler, B.L., Penrod, S.D. and Dexter, H.R. (1989) The eyewitness, the expert psychologist and the jury. *Law and Human Behaviour*, 13 (3).

Dion, K.K., Berscheid, E. and Walster, E. (1972). What is beautiful is good. *Journal of Personality and Social Psychology*, 24, 285–90.

Dooley, E. (1990) Prison suicide in England and Wales, 1972–87. *British Journal of Psychiatry*, 156, 40–5.

Eberhardt, J.L., Goff, P.A., Purdie, V.J. and Davies, P.G. (2004) Seeing Black: Race, crime, and visual processing. *Journal of Personality and Social Psychology*, 87, 876–93.

Eberhardt, J.L., Davies, P.G., Purdie-Vaughns, V.J. and Johnson, S.L. (2006) Looking deathworthy – perceived stereotypicality of black defendants predicts capital-sentencing outcomes. *Psychological Science*, 17 (5), 383–86.

Farrington, D.P., Ditchfield, J., Howard, P. and Joliffe, D. (2002). Two intensive regimes for young offenders: a follow-up evaluation. *Home Office Research, Development and Statistics Directorate, Research Findings*, 163, 1–4. (Cited from Donald, M. and Ellerby-Jones, L. (2011) *OCR A2 Psychology Key Studies Companion*, pp. 54–5. London: Hodder Education.)

Farrington, D.P., Coid, J.W., Harnett, L.M., Jolliffe, D., Soteriou, N., Turner, R.E. and West, D.J. (2006a) Criminal careers up to age 50 and life success up to age 48: new findings from the Cambridge Study in Delinquent Development. *Home Office Research and Statistics Directorate, Home Office Research Study 299*. London: Home Office

Farrington, D.P., Coid, J.W., Harnett, L.M., Jolliffe, D., Soteriou, N., Turner, R.E. and West, D.J. (2006b). Criminal careers and life success: new findings from the Cambridge Study in Delinquent Development. *Home Office Research and Statistics Directorate, Home Office Findings 281*. London: Home Office

Fishter, R.P., Geiselman, R.E. and Amador, M. (1989) Field test of the cognitive interview: enhancing the recollection of the actual victims and witnesses of crime. *Journal of Applied Psychology*, 74 (5), 722–7.

Frowd, C., Bruce, V., McIntyre, A. and Hancock, P. (2007) The relative importance of external and internal features of facial composites. *British Journal of Psychology*, 98, 61–77.

Gillis, C.A. and Nafekh, M. (2005) The impact of community-based employment on offender reintegration. *The Forum for Corrections*, 17 (1), 10–5. Prison Reform Trust (2007).

Gudjohnsson, G.H. and Mackeith, J.A.C. (1990) A proven case of false confession: psychological aspects of the coerced-compliant type. *Medicine, Science and the Law*, 30, 329–35.

Gudjohnsson, G.H. and Bownes, I. (2002) The attribution of blame and type of crime committed: data for Northern Ireland. *Journal of Forensic Psychiatry*, 2 (3), 337–41.

Gross, R. (2010) *The Science of Mind and Behaviour* (6th edn.), p. 756. London: Hodder Education.

Haney, C. and Zimbardo, P. (1998) The past and future of US prison policy, 25 years after the Stanford Prison Experiment. *American Psychologist*, 53 (7), 709–27.

Harrower, J. (2001) *Crime – Psychology in Practice*. London: Hodder Arnold. (Harrower cites Audit Commission, 1996, as source.)

Hastie, R., Penrod, S.D. and Pennington, N. (1983) *Inside the Jury*. Cambridge, Mass.: Harvard University Press.

Inbau, F., Reid, J. and Buckley, J. (1986) *Criminal Interrogation and Confessions* (3rd edn.). Baltimore: Williams & Wilkins.

Inbau, F.E. (1999) Police interrogation – a practical necessity. *Journal of Criminal Law and Criminology*, 89 (4), 1403–12.

Ireland, J. (2004) Anger management therapy with young male offenders: an evaluation of treatment outcome. *Aggressive Behaviour*, 30, 174–85.

Kohlberg, L. (1963) The development of children's orientations towards a moral order: sequence in the development of moral thought. *Human Development*, 6, 11–13. (NB. reprinted in 2008, *Human Development*, 51, 8–20)

Loftus, E.F. and Mackworth, N.H. (1978) Cognitive determinants of fixation location during picture viewing. *Journal of Experimental Psychology: Human Perception and Performance*, 4, 565–572. (Cited from Loftus, E.F., Loftus, G.R. and Messo, J. (1987) Some facts about weapon focus. *Journal of Law and Human Behaviour*, 11 (1), 55–62.)

Loftus, E.F., Loftus, G.R. and Messo, J. (1987) Some facts about weapon focus. *Journal of Law and Human Behaviour*, 11 (1), 55–62.

Mair, G. and May, C. (1997) Offenders on Probation. *Home Office Research and Statistics Directorate, Research Study 167*. London: Home Office.

Mann, S., Vrij, A. and Bull, R. (2004) Detecting true lies: police officers' ability to detect suspects' lies. *Journal of Applied Psychology*, 89(1), 137–49.

Moscovici, S. (1985) Social influence and conformity. In G. Lindzey and E. Aronson (eds.) *Handbook of Social Psychology* (3rd edn.). New York: Random House.

Nemeth, C. and Wachtler, J. (1974) Creating the perceptions of consistency and confidence: a necessary condition for minority influence. *Sociometry*, 37 (4), 529–40.

Pennington, N. and Hastie, R. (1988). Explanation-based decision-making: effects of memory structure on judgement. *Journal of Experimental Psychology, Learning and Memory and Cognition*, 14 (3), 521–33.

Penrod, S. and Cutler, B. (1995) Witness confidence and witness accuracy: assessing their forensic relation. *Psychology, Public Policy and Law*, 1 (4), 817–45.

Pickel, K.L. (1995) Inducing jurors to disregard inadmissible evidence a legal explanation does not help. *Law and Human Behaviour*, 19 (4).

Price, W.H., Strong, J.A., Whatmore, P.B. and McClemont, W.F. (1966) Criminal patients with XYY sex-chromosome complement. *The Lancet*, 1, 565–6. (Cited from Harrower, J. (2001) *Crime – Psychology in Practice*. London: Hodder Arnold.)

Raine, A. (2002) The role of prefrontal deficits, low autonomic arousal and early health factors in the development of anti-social and aggressive behaviour in children. *Journal of Child Psychology and Psychiatry*, 43 (4), 417–34.

Reicher, S. and Haslam, S.A. (2006) Rethinking the psychology of tyranny. The BBC Prison Study. *British Journal of Social Psychology*, 45, 1–40.

Ross, D.F., Hopkins, S., Hanson, E., Lindsay, R.C.L., Hazen, K. and Eslinger, T. (1994) The impact of protective shields and videotape testimony on conviction rates in a simulated trial of child sexual abuse. *Law and Human Behaviour*, 18 (5), 553–66.

Sherman, L.W. and Strang, H. (2007) *Restorative Justice – the Evidence*. London: Smith Institute.

Sutherland, E.H. (1947) *Principles of Criminology*. Chicago: Lippincott.

Vrij, A. and Mann, S. (2001) Who killed my relative? Police officers' ability to detect real-life high-stake lies. *Psychology, Crime and Law*, 7, 119–32.

Vrij, A. (2000) cited from Vrij, A. and Mann, S. (2001) Who killed my relative? Police officers' ability to detect real-life high-stake lies. *Psychology, Crime and Law*, 7, 119–32.

Wheatley, M. (2007) Needles help beat drug addiction. HM Prison Service and Cambridge University Institute of Criminology. Source: www.hmprisonservice.gov.uk/prisoninformation/prisonservicemagazine. (NB. Magazine ceased publication in 2009; copies may be available from The National Archives: http://webarchive.nationalarchives.gov.uk)

Wikström, P-O. & Tajfel, H. (2003) Findings from the Peterborough Youth Study. Available at http://www.scopic.ac.uk/StudiesPADS.html

Witkin, H.A., Mednick, S.A., Schulsinger, F., Bakkestrom, E., Christiansen, K.O., Goodenough, D.R., Hirschorn, K., Lundsteen, C., Owen, D.R., Philip, J. Rubin, D.B. and Stocking, M.M. (1976) Criminality in XYY and XXY men. *Science*, 193, 547–55. (Cited from Harrower, J. (2001) *Crime – Psychology in Practice*. London: Hodder Arnold.)

Wilson, M. and Daly, M. (1985) Competitiveness, risk-taking, and violence: the young male syndrome. *Ethology and Sociobiology*, 6, 59–73.

Wilson, M. and Daly, M. (1997) Life expectancy, economic inequality, homicide and reproductive timing in Chicago neighbourhoods. *British Medical Journal*, 314, 1271.

Yochelson, S. and Samenow, S. (1976) *The Criminal Personality*. New York: Jason Aronson.

Yochelson, S. and Samenow, S. (1984) *Inside the Criminal Mind*. New York: Random House. (Cited from Lintern, F., Stapleton, M. and Williams, L. (2004) *Study Guide for OCR Psychology: A2 Level*. London: Hodder & Stoughton.)

Health and clinical

Bandura, A. and Adams, N.E. (1977) Analysis of self-efficacy theory of behavioural change. *Cognitive Therapy and Research*, 1 (4), 287–310.

Beck, A. T. (1961) A systematic investigation into depression. *Comprehensive Psychiatry*, 2, 162–70.

Becker, H. (1978) Compliance with a medical regimen for asthma: a test of the Health Belief Model. *Public Health Reports*, 268–77.

Budzynski, T., Stoya, J., Adler, C., and Mullaney D.J. (1973) EMG biofeedback and tension headache: a controlled outcome study. *Psychosomatic Medicine*, 35 (6), 484–96.

Bulpitt, C.J. and Fletcher, A.E. (1988) Importance of well-being to hypertensive patients. *The American Journal of Medicine*, 84 (1B), 40–6.

Cowpe, C. (1989) Chip pan fire prevention 1976–1988. In C. Channer (ed) *Television Advertising Case Histories*, London: Cassell.

Danneburg, A.L., Gelen, A.C., Beilenson, P.L., Wilson, M.H. Joffe, A. (1993) Bicycle helmet laws and educational campaigns: an evaluation of strategies to increase children's helmet use. *American Journal of Public Health* 83 (5), 667–74.

DiNardo, P.A. (1998) Generalized Anxiety Disorder. In T.A. Widiger, A.J.Frances, H.A. Pincus, R. Ross, M.B. First and W.W. Davis (eds), *DSM-IV Sourcebook*, 259–66. Washington DC: American Psychiatric Association.

Ford, M.R. and Widiger, T.A. (1989) Sex bias in the diagnosis of histrionic and antisocial personality disorders. *Journal of Consulting and Clinical Psychology*, 57 (2), 301–5.

Foundation, Mental Health. *Mental Health Foundation* (2001) http://www.mentalhealth.org.uk/help-information/mental-health-statistics/ (accessed 16 November 2011).

Freeman, D., Garety, P.A. Kuipers, E., Fowler, D. and Bebbington P.E. (2002) A cognitive model of persecutory delusions. *British Journal of Clinical Psychology*, 41, 331–47.

Frith, C.D. (1992) *The Cognitve Neuropsychology of Schizophrenia*. Hove: LEA.

Geer, J.H. and Maisel, E. (1972) Evaluating the effects of the prediction-control confound. *Journal of Personality and Social Psychology*, 23 (3), 314–19.

Gottesman I.J. and Shields, J. (1976) A critical review of recent adoption, twin and family studies of shizophrenia: behavioural genetics perspectives. *Schizophrenia Bulletin*, 2 (3), 360–401.

Heffner, C.L. *AllPsych online* (2004) http://allpsych.com/disorders/ (accessed 11 November 2011).

Holmes, T.H. and Rahe, R.H. (1967) The social readjustment scale. *Journal of Psychosomatic Research*, 11 (1), 213–8.

Janis, I.L. and Feshbach, S. (1953) Effects of fear-arousing communications. *The Journal of Abnormal and Social Psychology*, 48 (1), 78–92.

Johansson, G., Aronsson, B.O. and Lindstrom (1978) Social psychological and neuroendocrine stress reactions in highly mechanised work. *Ergonomics*, 21 (8), 583–99.

Kane, J.M. Rifkin,A., Quitkin, F., Nayak, D. and Ramos-Lorenzi, J. (1982) Fluphenazine vs placebo in patients with remitted acute first-episode schizophrenia. *Archives of General Psychiatry* 39, 70–3.

Kanner, A.D., Coyne, J.C. and Schaefer, C. (1981) Comparison of two modes of stress measurement: daily hassles and uplifts versus major life events. *Journal of Behavioural Medicine*, 4 (1), 1–39.

Karp, J.F. and Frank, E. (1995) Combination therapy and the depressed woman. *Depression*, 3, 91–8.

Lam, D.H., Watkins, E.R., Hayward, P., Bright, J., Wright, K., Kerr, N., Parr-Davis, G. and Sham, P. (2003) A randomised controlled study of cognitive therapy for relapse prevention for bipolar affective disorder. *Archives of General Psychiatry*, 60 (2), 145–52.

Lewinsohn, P.M. and Libet, J. (1972) Pleasant events, activity schedules and depressions. *Journal of Abnormal Psychology*, 79 (3), 291–5.

Lewinsohn, P.M., Youngren, M.A. and Grosscup, S.J. (1979) Reinforcement and depression. In R.A. Dupue (ed) *The psychobiology of depressive disorders: Implications for the effects of stress*, 291–316. New York: Academic Press.

Lewisohn, P.M., Clarke, G.N., Hops, H. and Andrews, J. (1990) Cognitive behavioural treatment for depressed adolescents. *Behaviour Therapy* 21, 385–401.

Liberman, R.P. (1982) Assessment of social skills. *Schizophrenia Bulletin*, 8 (1), 62–84.

Liebowitz, M.R., Gorman, J.M., Fyer, A.J., Campeas, R., Levin, A.P., Sandberg, D. Hollander, E., Papp, L. and Goetz, D. (1988) Pharmacotherapy of social phobia: an interim report of a placebo controlled comparison of phenelzine and atenolol. *Journal of Clinical Psychiatry*, 49 (7), 252–7.

Lustman, P.J., Freedland, K.E., Griffith, L.S. and Clouse, R.E. (2000) Fluoxetine for depression in diabetes: a randomized double-blind placebo-controlled trial. *Diabetes Care*, 23 (5), 618–23.

Macleod, S.A. (2008) *Simply Psychology*. http://www.simplypsychology.org/abnormal-psychology.html (accessed 28 October 2011).

Maher, B.A. (1988) Anomalous experiences and delusional thinking. In T.F. Oltmanns and B.A. Maher (eds) *Delusional Beliefs*, 15–33, New York: Wiley.

McGrath, T., Tsui, E., Humphries, S. and Yule, W. (1990) Successful treatment of a noise phobia in a nine-year-old girl with systematic desensitisation in vivo. *Educational Psychology*, 10 (1), 79–83.

Meichenbaum, D.H. (1972) Cognitive modification of test anxious college students. *Journal of Consulting and Clinical Psychology*, 39 (3), 370–80.

Ohman, A. Erixon, G. and Lofberg, I. (1975) Phobias and preparedness: phobic versus neutral pictures as conditioned stimuli for human autonomic responses. *Journal of Abnormal Psychology*, 84 (1), 41–5.

Ost, L.G. and Westling, B. (1995) Applied relaxation vs cognitive behaviour therapy in the treatment of panic disorder. *Behaviour Research and Therapy*, 33 (2), 145–58.

Paul, G.L. and Lentz, R.J. (1977) *Psychosocial Treatment of Chronic Mental Patients*. Cambridge, Mass: Harvard University Press.

Rosenhan, D.L. (1973) On being sane in insane places. *Science*, 179 (70), 250–58.

Rosenhan, D.L. and Seligman, M.E.P. (1995) Defining abnormality. *Abnormal Psychology*, 3, New York: Norton.

Rosenstock, I.M. (1974) Historical origins of the health belief model. *Health Education Monographs*, 2 (4), 328–35.

Rotter, J.B. (1966) Generalized expectancies for internal versus external control of reinforcement. *Psychological Monographs: General and Applied*, 1–27.

Rush, A.J., Hollon, S.D. Beck, A. and Kovacs, M. (1978) Must pharmacology fail for cognitive therapy to succeed? *Cognitive Therapy and Research*, 2 (2), 199–206.

Sensky, T., Turkington, D., Kingdon, D. Scott, J.L., Scott, J., Siddle, R., O'Carroll, M. and Barnes, T.R.E. (2000) A randomised controlled trial of cognitive behavioural therapy for persistent symptoms in schizophrenia resistant to medication. *Archives of General Psychiatry*, 57 (2), 115.

Strunk, D.R., Brotman, M.A. and DeRubeis, R.J. (2010) The process of change in cognitive therapy for depression: predictors of early inter-session symptom gains. *Behaviour Research and Therapy*, 48 (7), 499–506.

Sullivan, P.F, Neale, M.C. and Kendler, K.S. *Genetic epidemiology of major depression: review and meta-analysis*. American Journal of Psychiatry. *Psychiatry Online* (1 October 2000) http://ajp.psychiatryonline.org/article.aspx?articleID=174362 (accessed 2 November 2011)

Szasz, T. (1960) The myth of mental illness. *The American Psychologist*, 15 (2), 113–8.

Watson, J.B. and Rayner, R. (1920) Conditioned emotional reactions. *Journal of Experimental Psychology*, 3 (1), 1–14.

Watt, P.M., Clements, B., Devadson, S.G. and Chaney, G.M. (2003) Funhaler spacer: improving adherence without compromising on delivery. *Archives of Diease in Childhood*, 88, 579–81.

Waxler-Morrison, N., Hislop, T.G., Mears, B. and Kan, L. (1991) Effects of social relationships on survival for women with breast cancer: a prospective study. *Social Sciences Medicine*, 33 (2), 177–83.

Sport and exercise

Allport, F.H. and Odbert, H.S. (1936) Trait names: a psycho-lexical study. *Psychological Monographs*, 47, 211.

Bandura, A., Ross, D. and Ross, S.A. (1961) Transmission of aggression through imitation of aggressive models. *Journal of Abnormal and Social Psychology*, 63, 575–82.

Bandura, A. and Adams, N. (1977) Analysis of self-efficacy theory of behavioural change. *Cognitive Therapy and Research*, 1, (4), 287–310.

Beck, A.T., Ward, C.H., Mendelson, M., Mock, J. and Erbaugh, J. (1961) An inventory for measuring depression. *Archives of General Psychiatry*, 4, 53-63.

Berkowitz, L. and Geen, R.G. (1966) Film violence and the cue properties of available targets. *Journal of Personality and Social Psychology*, 3 (5), 525–30.

Bernstein, L., Henderson, B.E., Hanisch, R., Sullivan-Halley, J. and Ross, R.K. (1994) Physical exercise and reduced risk of breast cancer in young women. *Journal of the National Cancer Institute*, 86 (18), 1403–8.

Cannon, W.B. (1929) *Bodily changes in pain, hunger, fear and rage*. New York: Appleton-Century-Crofts.

Carron, A.V. (1982) Cohesiveness in sports groups: interpretations and considerations. *Journal of Sport Psychology*, 4, 123–38.